CLIFFORD A. COLE:
A Calming and Reasoned Spirit

Volume 6
MAKERS OF CHURCH THOUGHT SERIES

CLIFFORD A. COLE:
A Calming and Reasoned Spirit

BY GEOFFREY F. SPENCER

Herald Publishing House
Independence, Missouri

Other titles in the Makers of Church Thought Series:
F. Henry Edwards: Articulator for the Church
    by Paul M. Edwards
Evan Fry: Proclaimer of Good News
    by Alan D. Tyree
Roy A. Cheville: Explorer of Spiritual Frontiers
    by Henry K. Inouye Jr.
Arthur A. Oakman: An Artist with Words
    by Maurice L. Draper
Geoffrey F. Spencer: Advocate for an Enlightened Faith by Wayne Ham

Copyright © 1999
Herald Publishing House
Independence, Missouri

ISBN 0-8309-0845-5

Printed in the United States of America

02 01 00 99   1 2 3 4   12-059055

Preface and Acknowledgments

In the *Who's Who in America* the following statement accompanies the entry for Clifford Adair Cole:

> Everyone who thinks deeply must answer the question: "What is the ultimate reality undergirding the universe?" The answer is not found in proof but rather in faith. The struggle has led me to a profound and abiding faith in God.*

In this brief affirmation Clifford Cole has pointed to the foundation on which his life in the church, and his contribution to its thinking, has been shaped. As specified in Doctrine and Covenants 154:1 that contribution has been marked by a calming spirit and a reasoned approach, at a time when these gifts did indeed constitute a blessing to the church. At no time, however, did Clifford sacrifice the demands of integrity for the sake of a simplified understanding or a superficial peace. His thinking has ranged over a broad spectrum of theological issues and invariably called the Saints to an expanded understanding and commitment.

I have come to the conclusion that few tasks are more difficult than the attempt to plumb the thought of another individual and reproduce it with truthfulness and accuracy. Fortunately Clifford has been consistently available to offer his perspective and kindly advice when it was most needed. It has been a personal pleasure to work with him in an undertaking of this kind. I would like to think that this book is some small tribute for a person who has given no thought to his own aggrandizement during his long tenure as a significant leader in the life of the church.

A word about the format. In constructing this review I have also formed the opinion that few things are as lack-

---

*Who's Who in America, 53rd Edition, Vol. 1:844.

luster and tedious to read as a summarized statement of the writings of another. At least I came to this opinion very soon regarding my own abilities in my treatment of Clifford's Cole's work. For this reason I have relied heavily on direct quotations from Clifford's writings. The accompanying text has been added essentially to provide background and continuity in the treatment of the material. I trust that this has resulted in a helpful marriage of original text and supporting data.

Geoff Spencer

Table of Contents

Preface and Acknowledgments 5
Chapter 1: **A Minister in the Making** 9
Chapter 2: **The Years under Appointment** 15
              Reflections by Clifford Cole 15
              Observations by the Author 19
Chapter 3: **The Life of Faith** 23
              The Human Dilemma 25
              A Mature Faith 27
              Try the Spirits 29
              We Are What We Believe 31
Chapter 4: **By Study and Also by Faith** 35
              A Love for Graceland 36
              The Education of Children and Youth .. 36
              A Lifelong Advocate for Learning 38
              The Basic Beliefs Committee 39
              The Challenge of Education 40
              Education and Spiritual Maturity 42
Chapter 5: **The Body of Christ** 45
              Foundation, Apostasy, and Restoration
                Revisited 45
              The Nature of the Church 49
              The Great Divide 51
              The Church as Leaven 52
Chapter 6: **And Members in Particular** 59
              Children and Youth 59
              The World of the Student 61
              Women in Church and World 64
              Marriage and Family 67
Chapter 7: **Into All the World** 71
              The Changing Face of Evangelism 74
              The Church Expands Its Mission 76
              The Witnessing Congregation 78
              A Place for the Institution 80
Chapter 8: **From Isles and Continents Afar** 83
              To See with New Eyes 84

	When the Gospel Encounters Culture	85
	The Heart of the Gospel	88
	A New Appreciation for Culture	89
	Autonomy for Every Culture	91
	The Challenge of Pluralism	93
Chapter 9:	**The Cause of Zion**	97
	A Growing Symbol	98
	A Land of Promise?	101
	Agenda for a Growing Church	102
	Power in Gathering	104
	Facing the Future	106
Chapter 10:	**With Eyes on the Horizon**	109
	Our Opportunity for Greatness (1966)	109
	The Church of Jesus Christ Confronting Its Mission (1968)	111
	The Great Witnesses (1970)	113
	Called into This Time (1972)	115
	The Cause of Zion Today and Tomorrow (1974)	118
	On Being the Body of Christ (1976)	120
	On Choosing Life (1978)	122
	Poised between Eras (1980)	123
Chapter 11:	**The Prophetic View**	129
	The Prophets Spoke	129
	Prophecy and Presidency	132
	A Prophetic People	134
Chapter 12:	**In Retrospect**	139
Chapter 13:	**In Appreciation**	147
	Duane E. Couey	147
	J. C. Stuart	150
	Alan D. Tyree	152
	Maurice L. Draper	154
	Donald V. Lents	155
	Reed M. Holmes	157
	Howard S. Sheehy Jr.	158
	Lloyd B. Hurshman	159
Appendix:	**A Parable of Mission**	163
Bibliography		167

CHAPTER 1

A Minister in the Making

Weather records confirm that 1934 was a disastrous year in Wyoming for those who depended on favorable conditions in making their living. The shortage of water and the summer heat rendered conditions intolerable for the proper care of sheep and cattle. Clifford Cole was then eighteen years of age, working for $20 a month and room and board on a neighbor's property and raising a small flock of sheep of his own. The conditions forced him to sell his flock to the government; the animals were promptly slaughtered for their pelts.

As distressing as the climatic and economic conditions were in 1934, it was a time of significant decision for the young man. For some time, with the nation in the midst of a depression, he had been seriously reflecting on his future. With the encouragement of Lucile Hartshorne, the young woman he would soon marry, Clifford considered enrolling at Graceland College. With such earnings as he had been able to accumulate, augmented by the sale of his flock, he enrolled in the fall of that year as a pre-dental student and was one of the two students to graduate from that one-year course in 1935. His experience at Graceland was the first of several significant relationships that he would enjoy with the college in the years to come. Over the next two decades he would continue to cultivate an interest and aptitude for teaching, which would serve the church well.

The path had not been easy for Clifford Cole. He was born in Lamoni in 1915, where his father was a printer at

Herald Publishing House. However, when he was three the family heeded medical advice and moved to Wyoming where his father homesteaded and then ranched. By the time he was twelve he had been well exposed to ranching life. Due mainly to the insistence of his mother that he should receive a sound education, he moved to the town of Moorcroft in 1929 to attend high school. There he boarded with the family of the Presbyterian minister, the Reverend Elbert Nash.

Clifford was baptized in the Reorganized Church of Jesus Christ of Latter Day Saints Church as an eight-year-old-child, although the opportunities for participation in congregational life were sparse. While attending the Presbyterian church during his stay with the Nash family, several profound experiences impressed themselves on his consciousness. Without attempting to prejudice his thinking, the Reverend Nash encouraged him to explore his religious convictions, and to subject them to careful scrutiny. This was a time when the young man found himself raising questions about some of the traditional RLDS beliefs, yet affirming his appreciation for the faith into which he had been born. In this way he was able to be free from both destructive criticism on the one hand and naïve faith on the other.

It could well be said that this stance—of informed reason wedded to appreciative affirmation—formed the foundation of Clifford Cole's ministry throughout his life. Of that crucial time in his growing years, he has said:

> While I experienced the Spirit of God in worshiping among them [the Presbyterians], I knew that I had also experienced that in worshiping among Latter Day Saints.... The question then was, "What is happening now?" And I recognized that God was working among Latter Day Saints. I felt he was recognizing them and therefore they were a perfectly valid church. I recognized also that in the Latter Day Saint church was where the people lived that I loved. I had grown

up among them, I understood them, and I said: "Well, whether Joseph Smith actually had all the experiences or not, this is still where I want to be, and as I live in the context of the church, and as time goes along I'll probably come to know better than I do now what to believe and what not to believe about the early history of the church." And so that was the way I came back into my real activity in the church.[1]

When asked whether these were fairly unusual conclusions to be arrived at under the circumstances Clifford replied:

Yes. I think I must have been among a very few people who would, in that period of the church's history, be coming up with that kind of conclusion. As a result, there were times when I found it very difficult to talk to anyone because there wasn't anyone who really understood.

Upon returning from his one year at Graceland, Clifford attended a reunion at Devil's Tower, Wyoming, and there had an experience that turned his mind increasingly in the direction of a life's calling to ministry and away from the prospect of continuing his training in dentistry. That same year he was ordained to the office of priest, and the following year he and Lucile were married. Lucile was already teaching in a rural school and Clifford secured a provisional certificate in Wyoming that would enable him to fund further education, first at the University of Wyoming and subsequently at Graceland College.

In 1940 Clifford was asked to run the store where he had been working, with Lucile's assistance. After several months, with the help of his father, he purchased the store. Not too long after, however, the Coles sold the store and in the fall of 1941 Clifford enrolled in Graceland again. In 1942 he earned an associate's degree from Graceland and stayed on to teach in Lamoni. This was a particularly important period in the formative years of one who was to bring a profoundly influential leadership in the life of the church. Still drawn by the vision of a call to ministry, though as yet unspecified, Clifford appreciated his association with such men as Roy Cheville, Gustave Plotts, Gene Closson, and Ed Gleazer Jr., then the Lamoni Stake president. Lamoni congregation offered a lively and progressive environment for the young elder (he had been ordained in 1939), enriched by the fact that the college community participated in the life of the congregation.

Completing a two-year course in twelve months, Clifford received a bachelor's degree in education from Central Missouri State Teachers' College in 1944, and then returned to Lamoni. With the nation at war, he was drafted and reported for service. The young draftee considered the merchant marine service, and then applied to serve as a chaplain. By chance, the First Presidency, whose clearance would have been required, were out for the summer, and his request was not acted upon. However, he received a deferment and returned to Lamoni to teach. He was called up again in 1945, but was in Leavenworth taking the physical when the war in Europe ended, and he was again given a deferment.

With a clearer picture of where he desired to serve, Clifford completed the papers applying for General Church appointment in the spring of 1945 but heard nothing from the church in response to his application. Because the time had passed for signing a contract to teach in Lamoni, he made arrangements to accept a teaching post in Latin America. Then, at the 1946 General Conference he happened to encounter F. Henry Edwards, with whom he shared his interest in church appointment. Edwards explained that due to the death of President Frederick M. Smith and the subsequent need for reorganizing the First Presidency, such matters had been set aside temporarily. He was encouraged to wait until he heard something definite before moving to Latin America.

Clifford then taught temporarily at Bellevue in eastern Iowa. After just one month he received a letter from the Joint Council approving his appointment, and at the end of the school year, in May 1947, he commenced his full-time ministry for the church. His first assignment was as president of the Northwest Iowa District. In 1951 he was ordained to the office of high priest. During the summer of 1951 a staffing emergency arose at Graceland, and Clifford accepted a leave of absence to serve as dean of students at the college. He resumed church appointment in June 1953 and directed the children's work within the Department of Religious Education. It then seemed most natural, as the culmination of years of dedicated preparation, that he should be appointed director of the department at the 1954 General Conference.

It seemed equally appropriate that Clifford should be called to the Council of Twelve in 1958, along with his close friend, Charles Neff, who had entered appointment about the same time. In 1964, although one of the younger apostles in seniority, his devotion and leadership skills had so commended him to his brethren that he was elected president of the council, a responsibility he was to carry until being honorably released from church appointment in 1980.

Notes

1. An Oral History, prepared under the supervision of the History Commission and recorded by Keith Henry (1980), 5.

CHAPTER 2

The Years under Appointment

Reflections by Clifford Cole

Lucile and I entered church appointment with a strong belief that we were committing our lives to a lifelong ministry under the leadership of the church. We never considered leaving church appointment to serve in any other vocation. However, we were very aware that the time might come when the financial condition of the church or unforeseen circumstances might require the church to release us as it had done in the severe depression of the 1930s. As a result both Lucile and I kept our contact with the teaching profession up to date.

Our first assignment as an appointee family was in the Northwest Iowa District. It was the intention of the Joint Council that I should serve as district president. When the next district conference was held, Apostle D. T. Williams presented my name as the nominee, supported by Brother Guy Johnson, the incumbent district president, and I was elected. Brethren Johnson and Walter Weldon were sustained as counselors. This team of the apostle-in-charge, the district presidency, the district bishopric, and seventy worked together, making the first years of our appointee life both very enjoyable and fruitful.

I did, however, immediately face a rather severe problem. At a district reunion held at Woodbine, Iowa, a couple of years before we arrived, three well-known visiting church leaders had teamed together to bring "spiritual" ministry to those in attendance. Because the Saints were always hoping the leaders would exercise the gifts of the Spirit in bringing what they believed was a "prophetic message" from the Lord, these leaders had brought such messages.

The essential impact of the messages was to warn the Saints that a terrible famine was about to come on them and that they should prepare for their own safety and have food for their neighbors, because little children would be crying for a crust of bread. The Saints felt the "gift" was so powerfully given and validated by the apostle present that they immediately began to store food in preparation for the famine. Unfortunately the persons bringing the so-called spiritual gift also said that the famine would be at its worst right at the time we arrived for our assignment. Contrary to their expectations for that year [1947] the crops were abundant and economic conditions relatively good. Many of the Saints were disillusioned; their faith in spiritual gifts and trusted church leadership was shattered.

As the new district president the need to help people work the problem through occupied much of my time. It also caused me to spend considerable time studying through the nature of numinous spiritual experience. It brought about a spiritual maturation that has helped me throughout my ministry.

Because Lucile and I were both schoolteachers I was attracted early on as an appointee to the needs of the children and youth. Soon after I became district president we wrote to all the branch presidents and asked for the names, birthdays, and addresses of the children who were either members of the RLDS Church or were attending activities, even if their families were not church members. We then sent birthday cards to each child on his or her birthday. Before going into the district to visit any area I reviewed the names of the children living there so I could call them by name and talk with them about the things they were doing. I then worked with the children's leaders to set up and, if possible, help with the summer vacation Bible schools. In some branches, if possible, an attempt was made to prepare children for baptism through the ministry offered in these vacation programs. Along with Brother Charles Neff, who was president of the Northeast Nebraska District, we organized and held summer camps for our junior high and senior high young people. Several of the women were also interested in organizing Skylark and Oriole girls' groups in some of the branches. These were especially helpful in attracting participation in church activities from non-RLDS homes.

We did try to minister to all of our Saints and especially help the two members of the Quorum of Seventy assigned to our district in their missionary work. Nevertheless it did seem to me that many opportunities to reach adults and unite families grew out of our outreach to children. When I observed children coming from homes of inactive or nonmember parents, it was my custom to ask the children if I could visit their homes. When the invitation to visit was extended I would, if it seemed appropriate, inform the parents that I observed that their child was becoming active and interested in our church but that we had a church policy against baptizing or unduly influencing a child to become a member without first receiving parental consent. This often led to a conversation in which I suggested that it would be helpful for us to have some cottage meetings in the home. After such meetings it was not unusual for the nonmember parent or parents to ask to be baptized with their child, whereby families could be united.

It is perhaps sufficient for me to say that I found ministry to children and young people to be very fruitful. Some dying branches were literally revived in this way.

On an August afternoon in 1951 I received a phone call from President F. Henry Edwards. As I answered the phone he said; "Clifford, are you standing up?" When I answered affirmatively he replied: "Well, sit down, I have a surprising question for you." He went on to tell me that Graceland College had an emergency need for a dean of students immediately and had asked the First Presidency if I could be given a leave of absence from church appointment to serve in this responsibility until they could employ another person to fill the vacancy. President Edwards asked me to meet him the next day at Graceland to talk about it. In a matter of hours I needed to transfer my responsibilities for the reunion of the Woodbine District, which was only a week away. Brother Charles Neff would assume this responsibility while I got ready to drive to Lamoni. The net result of the interview at Graceland was a leave of absence from church appointment and a very hurried move to Lamoni where I accepted responsibility as dean of students for the college. That responsibility continued for two years until Graceland employed Dr. Harold Condit to succeed me.

We then returned to active church appointment and I was assigned to the Department of Religious Education as director of children's ministry. Apostle Reed Holmes was the director of the department, but after I had served one year in the area of children's work, Apostle Holmes was given a field assignment and I was named director. We were in the midst of developing a curriculum for the church schools and it appeared to me at that time that my contribution to the church would be in the educational field. I also realized that even though my background and training were in education I needed much more training in curriculum construction to be able to lead the church in the Department of Religious Education. Particularly I would need to become a more capable educator if I expected to attract the quality I needed to bring into the department. Persons of quality were not going to work under the leadership of one less capable than they. After discussing this with President F.

Henry Edwards I enrolled at the University of Missouri–Kansas City on a part-time basis and set as a goal achieving a Ph.D. with a major in curriculum construction and a minor in theology.

I had just finished getting the final phase of the doctoral program approved and my doctoral committee established when President Israel A. Smith was killed in an automobile accident and I was given a strong feeling that I would never get to finish my doctoral degree. To some extent I felt rebellious that the goal I had defined for making a contribution to the church in the educational field appeared to be slipping away from me.

That summer was a trying time for me. I did, however, enroll in the university course set up in my program, but when the General Conference of the church met in October 1958, I was called to be a member of the Council of Twelve. I accepted the change and ended my plans for becoming a leader in the church's educational mission. I was assigned to Michigan and Ontario and dropped my doctoral program. The remaining years of my appointee ministry were in the Council of Twelve. In March 1979 I suffered a mild stroke. President Wallace B. Smith visited me in the hospital, and as a result of our conversation both of us knew I should be released from the Council of Twelve at the 1980 Conference. My service under the leadership of President W. Wallace Smith and Wallace B. Smith as well as with the other members of the Joint Council will always bring treasured memories to me. The fellowship of the Saints and the warm supportive relationships with other companions of the Joint Council and appointee force will always be a memory to cherish.

Observations by the Author

I knew Clifford Cole by reputation for several years before making his personal acquaintance after being assigned to the

Department of Religious Education, where Clifford was well known and highly respected. My respect was deepened as I had the opportunity to work with Clifford as a member of the Basic Beliefs Committee for a number of years. I appreciated Clifford as a minister who exerted a profound influence on the forward movement of the church during the decades of what might well have been the most significant period in its history to that point. The fact that Clifford's leadership was expressed in a notably quiet and unassuming manner did not in the least diminish its effect. Although earlier in this chapter he suggested that his entry into the Council of Twelve put an end to his educational leadership in the church, that is true only in a formal sense. Indeed his influence on the educational growth of the church was singularly effective throughout his entire life under appointment.

Clifford's recollections of his early years, both before and during church appointment, are noteworthy in that they signal gifts and priorities that were evident not only then, but foundational throughout his entire ministerial career. His concern that the Saints cultivate a fruitful appreciation of the life of the Spirit shows through his treatment of the problem encountered early in his first assignment and discussed early in the chapter. His interest and concern for young people, manifested in his work in northwest Iowa, was apparent in the many articles he wrote for *Guidelines for Leadership* and other church leadership journals between 1953 and 1958. A strong commitment to missionary outreach served him well as a member of the chief missionary quorum of the church in the ensuing years.

Although Clifford's recollections moved quickly through the years after his call into the Council of Twelve, the range of his special assignments signified a broad and significant contribution to the church. They can only be summarized briefly here:

- Commissioner of Education (1963–66)
- Basic Beliefs Committee (1960–70); chairperson (1966–70)
- Commissioner of Cultural Crises (1968–70)
- Council of Twelve Apostles (1958–80); president (1964–80)
- Director of Field Ministries (1970–79)
- Chairman, Higher Education Advisory Council (1980–82)
- Consultant to the First Presidency (1980–82)
- F. Henry Edwards Chair of Religious Studies at Graceland College (1982–83)

The books and study materials authored by Clifford Cole invariably ventured upon new understandings, while at the same time preserving a strong pastoral sensitivity to the needs of the membership. His leadership of the Basic Beliefs Committee before and during the time of the publication of *Exploring the Faith* (1970 edition) as well as his significant role in the Joint Council Seminars, which were exploring broader perceptions of the nature and mission of the church, were of crucial importance. It is the judgment of a number of contemporaries that the degree of unified commitment to the expansion of the church demonstrated by the Council of Twelve was unprecedented in that quorum. This took place at a time when the church was moving more extensively into the nations of the world than it ever had before.

The following chapters are an attempt to identify and explore the predominant themes in Clifford Cole's extensive writings over a thirty-year period. Many of the source materials were originally presented as *Saints Herald* articles, World Conference sermons, or in special settings for leaders, while others were unpublished. Wherever possible, citations will be referenced, although several substantial papers cannot be identified either by date or occasion of their presentation. At best, such a brief review of Clifford's voluminous writings can only be sketchy, though I have endeavored to apply the principle of selectivity as faithfully as possible.

CHAPTER 3
The Life of Faith

Clifford Cole addressed a wide range of subjects, as witnessed by the extensive list of books, articles, and papers bearing his name over a period of thirty years. If one is to discern a central and basic theme to this large body of work, it would have to be the fundamental significance of faith, both for the individual believer and for the body of the church at large. Faith was given form and effect not only as an intellectual undertaking, as important as this element might be, but was an exercise of the whole person: mind, emotions, commitments, and in the final analysis, life as it is lived out in acknowledgment of and trust in God.

It is evident from his writings that almost without exception Clifford addressed issues he considered to be not only of interest, but of timely, even urgent importance. This is certainly true of his 1956 publication, *Faith for New Frontiers.* The reason for this may be reflected in the Preface to the book *Exploring the Faith,* which he wrote as chairman of the Basic Beliefs Committee some years later in 1970. Here he wrote:

> Faith increasingly has been assaulted by various theological winds. Many of the old structures of belief have not been able to accommodate themselves to the dynamic developments of today. As a church we have not escaped that test....Ours is not a defense of some frozen form but a commitment to life—the life arising out of divinity which is expressed through the church, guiding, directing, and empowering her. This gives to the church flexibility to adjust herself to the call of God in the ever changing world.[1]

Clifford Cole entered World Church appointment at a time when the traditional faith of the church was undergoing possibly the most rigorous self-examination in its history. This was especially true insofar as *faith* was understood as the adherence to and defense of a body of doctrines considered necessary to "prove" the truth and authority of the Restoration movement.

In this 1956 work Clifford identified faith in two dimensions. The first element, identified as the **passive** aspect, related to "the body of beliefs and assumptions which are passed on by society from generation to generation" to provide stability and undergirding for that society. This was equally true whether applied to the larger cultural setting of any people or to the community of the church. Clifford did not dismiss such traditional assumptions, rather insisting that these should be constantly subjected to honest scrutiny and evaluation, lest they give way to naïve and superficial belief. It was a matter of concern to him that even the attempt to examine such beliefs was itself cause for alarm to many church members.

The second element, described as the **dynamic, qualitative** aspect, related to "the power to move out on new frontiers beyond the charted way." In both respects, the capacity to exercise a sound faith, either by way of affirming sound foundations or exploring new frontiers, lay in an unswerving trust in God as creator and sustainer, and in Jesus Christ as redeemer of humankind:

> When men are in turmoil within themselves, torn by conflicting values and trying to live up to the expectations of groups who demand of them conflicting allegiances and actions, the need is great in every heart to re-establish the deep conviction that God and his Son, Jesus Christ, are the almighty creators of heaven and earth and all that is in them. It is to God, and his Son, Jesus Christ, that honor and glory are due, and in this faith all other demands and loyalties recede into a perspective of true value.[2]

In light of the confusion and unrest that assailed many people, both in the larger society and in the church, Clifford saw the pressing need for such a faith in God, which would free people to explore new frontiers without yielding to disbelief on the one hand, or to superficial and unexamined belief on the other:

> Never has the need for such a faith been more desperate. The turmoil of our times leaves people grasping for some security, yet feeling that so much of what they once thought was solidly nailed down is now coming loose.... It is our hope that courageous men and women of our time will arise to grasp the outstretched hand of God, knowing that faith in God is not outgrown. It is the very essence of life itself.[3]

The Human Dilemma

The struggle for a significant (saving) faith takes on its shape from the peculiar—indeed the unique—nature of human beings:

> We must understand that we are the strangest of all God's creatures. While on the one hand we are animals with all of the drives, needs, and selfishness of animals, we are on the other hand gifted with intellect, sensitivity to beauty, and abilities to create both physically and spiritually in ways that go beyond any other creature.... We are tempted by the Divine, yet mired in the physical.[4]

The unique endowment of human beings beguiles them into the illusion that they can solve their problems unaided: "strong enough, wise enough, and good enough to master their own unsatisfactory situation." While this response may appear to offer some sense of self-sufficiency, it is short-lived and ultimately self-destructive. In this struggle is evident a universal hunger:

> In reality men can never be satisfied to live by bread alone, for they are impelled by intellectual and spiritual drives from within which make them struggle to know the meaning and purpose of life. Men yearn for a faith as inevitably as they breathe. When men lose their faith, the light within their souls goes out, and they face

a hopeless, senseless abyss which makes them afraid of each other and the world around them.[5]

It was Clifford's personal conviction that the path to freedom lay in a willingness to let go of the past, with its self-defeating struggles, and to accept the new life graciously extended through Jesus Christ. From this point of view, faith called for a bold renunciation of our former selves:

> Is there ever a man who doesn't at some time feel that he is a captive to his own past?... I should like to bear my testimony that the gospel of Jesus Christ has a message of hope for us in this predicament and that Christ can in the most practical ways help us free ourselves from the burden of past mistakes to be the kind of persons we ought to be.... We do not disown the past, or divorce ourselves from it, rather Christ takes all of it, even the evil part, and uses it to remake us into new persons. Jesus does not want us to drag our pasts along with us either to lament the evil or to parade our successes.... To be successful in saintly discipleship, we must believe that we can change and become new persons. In commonly used terms, we must have faith.[6]

At the same time it was extremely important, in Clifford's view, that letting go of the past not be understood as abandoning the memories and insights of the past. Whether one spoke of the broader culture or the history of the church, it was critical to be able to appreciate the heritage bequeathed us. The failure to do this amounted, in his view, to cultural amnesia. The contemporary folk wisdom tended to discount the past and to locate primary significance in the present moment. A sound faith could not be maintained if there was no perception of the contribution of the past upon which we stood:

> Let us suppose for a moment that we should all become amnesia victims and lose our memory of the past. What would such a catastrophe mean to us?... Although we are the beneficiaries of history, we cannot profit by the knowledge familiar to our forefathers if we neglect to acquaint ourselves with their experiences.... Through our knowledge of the past our wisdom and knowledge are increased.[7]

From this perspective, the traditions and history of the community of our predecessors were vital to an active faith. In the communal experience of worship, the sharing of the ordinances, and the ability to know how we got to be where we were, faith was nurtured:

> Our forms of worship are important to our faith...[and] they provide a means by which growing faith in God may be developed and nurtured.... A people with a vital living faith will be a people who intelligently recognize the great spiritual universality of God, but also cultivate the art of personal and congregational worship by which he becomes real, personal, and companionable. Intelligence on every level will find adequate expression of worship the key to faith.[8]

A Mature Faith

For better or for worse, human beings entered the contemporary world in which a bewildering variety of competing and often conflicting values clamored for their loyalties. Again, this was equally true of society at large, and of the religious environment. It was perhaps most painfully true within any single denomination:

> Today the world is in such a ferment.... The person who lives in our society moves among companions who are not agreed regarding their expectations of him.... A faith in conflict creates persons in conflict within themselves.... It is not surprising, then, that in our day there should be such wavering regarding standards of life, values worthy of achievement, and loyalties which claim our allegiance.[9]

The confusion arising from discordant voices was not only a problem to be faced by adults, but faced youth and children as well. From the very earliest years children were subjected to the substantial impact of the media, and if the parents had different religious commitments the uncertainty could be intensified. Upon moving out beyond the confines of the home they were exposed to yet another range of values. Further, in the modern world there had been a tremendous speed-up in the rapidity with which the undergirding faith of societies rose and fell.

It might be understandable that individuals would yearn for and be attracted by traditional values and simple formulations of faith, which might reduce the discomfort of inquiry and the uncertainty of facing the "new frontiers" to which the writer was drawing attention. Nevertheless, he saw no alternative if the objective was a strong and mature faith:

> One of the great dangers faced by every generation is the disposition to interpret faith as a kind of blind, unintelligent struggle to believe in God. Such an approach to life often places a premium on both ignorance and laziness. It reasons that it is not necessary for man to study, explore, and question; rather he should look to God for his answers and God will supply.... This has never been the position of the Restoration.... God does not rejoice in our ignorance nor our negligence. His instruction is "as all have not faith, seek ye diligently and teach one another words of wisdom...seek learning even by study, and also by faith" (Doctrine and Covenants 85:36a).[10]

Clifford was aware that the first portents of a so-called religious revival were to be seen in the United States. Such an outburst of religious fervor was not the first in the nation. On at least three previous occasions, separated by about seventy years and lasting for approximately forty years, strenuous efforts had been expended to restore the traditional faith and values of the people. The Restoration movement itself, founded during the second of these "Awakenings," was one of several groups committed to reviving primitive Christianity in its fullness and purity. The danger was that such a revival might invite people to embrace a simplified and shallow version of faith:

> It is of interest to note that ofttimes the practical interpretation given by popular writers has depicted faith as a kind of psychological cure-all. Many testimonies are given by people who have tried religion,

and as a result assert that after living by the power of positive thinking and the power of faith they have doubled their salary, won back their wife, and improved their health.... The very nature of such an approach, however, is still the approach of a magician. We would not at all deny that the person who develops an affirmative faith will be a better person. But we would suggest that a religious revival based on expectations that religion will get one financial gains, social prestige, and physical health is quite unsound. Its roots are shallow and one may expect that such faith will be short-lived.[11]

A mature faith was also essential to a people who undertook to share their faith with others. While this was true of any person who attempted to influence the faith of another, it was especially critical for members of the Restoration movement who endeavored to respond to the commitment of missionary vitality:

The unwise and immature Latter Day Saint may attack the faith of another, little realizing that his own faith is so immature that he has little of real worth to offer his friend. He who would change the faith of others must first plumb the depths of his own faith, testing it for truth and evaluating it for worth.... It is entirely possible for even Latter Day Saints to convert people to shallow understandings that soon wear thin and leave them desolate. Shallow conversion does an injustice to everyone concerned.[12]

Try the Spirits

Clifford was concerned that maturity should extend to the spiritual expressions of the Saints, especially with respect to what were referred to as the "spiritual gifts." The particular gifts enumerated by Paul in the New Testament had been venerated in the life of the church and were accorded high respect, sometimes without regard to their soundness. Although the Saints had been advised in Doctrine and Covenants 125:15 that a lack of wisdom and restraint in administering to the sick had been "a fruitful source of trouble," misuse of the gifts continued to confuse and disillusion members. Clifford himself had faced a serious problem growing out of the unwise expression of prophecy during his first assignment. Such expressions revealed a severe immaturity of faith, regardless of the well-meaning motivation behind their occurrence.

It was perhaps to be expected that the proliferation of the "charismatic" gifts in the wider Christian community should have repercussions among the Saints. At the request of the First Presidency, who saw "the possibility of distortions developing," Clifford, at the time president of the Quorum of Twelve Apostles, was asked to address the issue. The matter of excess or distortion in use of the spiritual gifts was a long-standing one:

> The problems of excesses and distortions in the expression (or alleged expression) of the Holy Spirit has continued down through the centuries. While we might speak about the evidence of this in other religious organizations, we are concerned here with our own movement.... It is always difficult to maintain a sound spiritual perspective, for while on the one hand we believe sincerely in the Holy Spirit as the personal presence and power of God at work in us and in the world, we are also aware that many have distorted, misinterpreted, and sometimes imitated the expressions of the Holy Spirit to the detriment of themselves and others.[13]

Clifford identified the gift of **discernment** as of primary importance, while acknowledging that this gift was itself subject to misuse. It was appropriate, therefore, to suggest some simple tests to evaluate spiritual expressions. These included a sense of awe, of one's own limitations, of God's drawing love, of an urgency to serve God, and being God-centered not ego-centered. The genuine experience of the Holy Spirit would never supercede the agency of the individual to cause that person's faculties and sense of accountability to be set aside. The prompting of the Holy Spirit would never sanction behavior of a questionable or indiscreet familiarity on the grounds that "love had given spiritual sanction to such conduct." In the final analysis,

Saints will be helped if they thoughtfully evaluate their charismatic experience in the light of the kinds of tests given above. It ought to be clear that all which parades under the name of the Holy Spirit is not genuine, and some of these are very destructive both to congregations and to individual members.[14]

We Are What We Believe

In affirming that faith is the foundation on which people build their lives, Clifford drew attention to Immanuel Kant's observation that the personality of an individual is like an inverted pyramid, resting on its apex. This represents the basic conviction and commitment shaping every other choice in life. It is clear that for the Christian, this foundation is the response in faith to the ultimacy of God:

> The apex upon which life rests may be called "our set of basic assumptions." These are referred to as "assumptions" because they can never be proved. We accept them on faith. We erroneously suppose at times that certain ways of life are based upon provable facts.... The basic principle upon which you and I build our lives, the compelling pinnacle of the pyramid, is a belief in God. We will accept this belief by a thrust of faith, and, having done so, we then find what Augustine meant when he said long ago, "I believe, that I may know."[15]

While there may be evidences to support one's faith, the yearning for externally verifiable proofs was ill-founded and eventually defeating. For some, it might appear then that the venture of faith was too much of an unfounded risk. How could one commit oneself to a fundamental commitment and course of action without knowing the answers, without a map delineating the precise standards and directions? Clifford recounted the experience of one man who, during a stimulating reunion class, realized his previous misunderstanding on a certain issue, but rejoiced that he had, as it were, come from darkness into light:

God can work with persons who know they do not have the final answers. Such people are willing to take Christ at his word when he invites them to ask, seek, and knock. These must not expect their answers to be delivered on a silver platter while they relax in the shade. The quest is open to the fearless, the energetic, the faithful, and especially to the humble. From such, God does not turn away. The awareness that we are in darkness is perhaps our best asset. It is this sense of what we may become that stirs us to struggle upward toward God.[16]

For many people, faced with the complexity of their life's situation, the "darkness," rather than being a stimulating challenge is a dreadful prospect. Given the tendency in this culture to praise performance, achievement, success, it is tempting to resort to activity as the way to hold confusion or uncertainty at arm's length. The oft-repeated injunction "Don't just stand there, do something" would seem to lend credence to the priority of activity over reflection. Nevertheless, Clifford lifted up the importance of reflection, even if it involved discomfort and struggle:

We live in a day when there are many who say, "It isn't what one believes that is important. It is what he does that matters." This is an appealing argument to many persons, but it is dangerously erroneous. Men are what they believe. One of the greatest hazards to modern-day society is to be found in the shallowness of men's faith. If we hope to save ourselves from chaos and strengthen others who are on sandy foundations, we must understand the faith upon which we build.[17]

Such a faith, in Clifford's view, was broadly based, and drew upon the totality of a person's resources, and those available to the disciple as a part of a worshiping fellowship:

Such a faith must minister to the souls of men, not alone because it stands the test of their curiosity and intellectual inquiry but because it ministers to the whole of life. It must stand the test of their emotions as they reach out for beauty and love. It must meet the test of abiding worship, for it is through active faith that they approach God and stand in the presence of the Holy...No amount of opposition, loss of possessions, or even persecution will permanently destroy our cause unless our people lose confidence in the basic undergirding faith itself.[18]

Clifford was under no illusion about the destructiveness of competing ideologies, nor about the seeming attractiveness of lesser commitments and allegiances. At the same time, out of his own abiding faith, he was able to challenge the Saints to rise to the quality of faith that contemporary society and church demanded:

> We have our idols and in one way or another we often sacrifice our lives and the lives of our children to them. Our idols take the form of trust in power, money, popular approval, and a host of other things that seem so real and firm. Like all idols, they block the way to God and sometimes it isn't until they are shattered before our eyes that we reach higher where, out beyond the idols of our day, we touch the hand of God. If this be so, let us not despair or disdain the chastening which forces us to reach up to God. Only let us reach, and having touched his hand, remember the injunction to Peter, "I have prayed for you, that your faith fail not; and when you are converted strengthen your brethren" (Luke 22:32).[19]

Notes

1. *Exploring the Faith: A Series of Studies in the Faith of the Church Prepared by a Committee on Basic Beliefs* (Herald House, 1970).
2. *Faith for New Frontiers* (Herald House, 1956), 28.
3. Ibid., Preface.
4. "What Does It Mean to Be Saved?" (undated paper), 1.
5. *Faith for New Frontiers*, 11–12.
6. "Apostle's Testimony," in *Restoration Witness* (April 1967).
7. *The Revelation in Christ*, 134–135.
8. *Faith for New Frontiers*, 138–139.
9. Ibid., 40–41.
10. Ibid., 93–94.
11. Ibid., 113.
12. Ibid., 77–78.
13. "Expressions of the Holy Spirit," in *Saints Herald* (January 1975), 11.

14. Ibid.
15. "The Nature of God," in *Facing Today's Frontiers*, edited by Department of Religious Education (1965), 30, 35.
16. *The Revelation in Christ*, 26.
17. *Faith for New Frontiers*, 152.
18. Ibid., 22, 66.
19. Ibid., 146.

CHAPTER 4

By Study and Also by Faith

When Clifford Cole introduced the work of the Basic Beliefs Committee published in the book *Exploring the Faith* (1970) he expressed both an invitation and a challenge that had become increasingly important for the church:

> The church must pay the price to be prophetic by entering the struggle for understanding and interpreting God's will in the midst of every generation. This means that we do not sit with hands folded, expecting God to do our work for us. Rather, like Oliver Cowdery, all of us are commanded to enter reverently but aggressively into the struggle.... There is no substitute for devoted study, worship, prayer, and hard work.[1]

The combination of elements identified above pointed to a fusion of faith and study as the foundation for the ministry of the church in the contemporary world. In Clifford's estimation, education was of the utmost importance, not primarily as an intellectual pursuit to satisfy curiosity or win personal aggrandizement, but as fundamental to mature faith and effective discipleship. His own journey had demonstrated a love and respect for education, often under circumstances that would have persuaded a lesser person to give up the struggle and seek the easier way. Yet Clifford persevered, both in the formal classroom of academic study and in the many opportunities for learning that otherwise presented themselves. In so doing, he became a noteworthy advocate for the value of learning "by study and also by faith."

A Love for Graceland

Clifford's respect for learning is symbolized in his association over the years with Graceland College, first as a student, then as dean of students when called upon to meet an emergency, and finally as a guest professor, filling the F. Henry Edwards Chair of Religious Studies in 1982–83. For more than forty years this relationship with the church's college was a mutually enriching one. It is interesting to note that both the first and the last of Clifford's writings to appear in the *Herald,* in 1942 and 1983, recounted experiences at Graceland. Of his earlier experience, at the time of graduation with an associate's degree, Clifford wrote:

> Now, however, as I approach the day of graduation from Graceland, I feel again as I did on that day of departing from home friends over seven years ago. There are a good many heart throbs connected with the realization of this thing I have anticipated so long. I am wondering *why* I ever worked so hard to achieve a goal that I now approach with such reluctance.[2]

This report reflected both the intensity of investment and the uncertainty at points along the way that had brought Clifford to that stage. Forty years later, writing as guest professor, he would write:

> I have feelings of warmth and friendship toward many fine instructors in good colleges and universities. However, just as I have driven by many houses of worship to attend a congregation of my own church, so I have passed by educational institutions which may have been closer or more economical in order to attend a college of my church. I have done this because I have felt it has been worth the extra effort and price in both cases.[3]

The Education of Children and Youth

Following a two-year term as dean of students at Graceland, Clifford was assigned to direct the children's division of the Department of Religious Education. He wrote a number of articles in church periodicals (especially *Guidelines to Leadership*) from 1953 to 1958, upholding the importance of children's education and providing practical guidance in a wide range of topics.

At the 1954 General Conference Clifford was assigned to direct the Department of Religious Education, and it was in this role that he continued to serve until called into the Council of Twelve in 1958. A major undertaking during this time was the development of plans for revising the church school curriculum for children and youth. Of this project, started in 1952 under the leadership of Reed Holmes, Clifford stated:

> We started out with raising questions about what kind of curriculum the church should have. And after considerable discussion, [we] came to kind of a simple statement which said: The kind of curriculum we should have is a curriculum that will help people become good Latter Day Saints. I think as a practical expression, it's worked out all right for us.... We soon began to describe curriculum as not just materials but an experience. We asked what are the kind of experiences and what are the kinds of materials needed to provide those experiences.[4]

A fundamental guideline for the materials produced was the balance between intellectual honesty for the truth as understood and pastoral concern for the Saints using the curriculum. This guideline Clifford explained as follows:

> I always took the position that we did not necessarily need to have to write in our material all of the controversial things that we knew to be true, but we would not put in our material anything we knew was untrue.... I was never willing to permit us to write something that I knew was wrong, and would, someday, have to be unlearned. And so, while we didn't necessarily write everything we knew, what we did write was to the best of our knowledge true and will stand up in years to come as persons grow in their faith.[5]

The major project was still taking shape when Clifford was called into the Council of Twelve. While in retrospect this would seem to have been a timely and appropriate call, it was not approached by the new apostle without mixed feelings:

> I felt that education was an area in which I had some skills and expertise to help in the church. In fact at the time I kind of saw that as being pretty much the major thrust of my ministry. I thought that I would probably continue in the department through the rest of my appointee life. I would have to say that I was a little bit disturbed when I first began to realize that my work in the department might end and I might go into another area of work. I didn't look forward to going into the Twelve at all [6]

A Lifelong Advocate for Learning

It must, however, be said that entry to the Council of Twelve did not mean an end to Clifford's interest in and contribution to the educational program of the church. Apart from serving as commissioner of education from 1963 to 1966 and chairman of the Higher Education Advisory Board (1980–1982), his subsequent participation on a number of special committees and as president of the Council of Twelve and director of Field Ministries exerted a beneficial impact on the way education was perceived and implemented throughout the church.

Clifford's interests and concerns were wide ranging. In a report issued shortly before he left the Department of Religious Education advances on a number of fronts were described. The *Oriole Girls' Handbook* had been extensively revised. New prebaptismal materials and a new three-year cycle of vacation church school and reunion materials had been completed for use with children. A new cycle of Zion's League annuals was developed. The God and Country program had been completed and a new manual on Scouting was in preparation. This was in addition to the new materials being developed for church school classes from primary through senior high.

Clifford saw the possibilities in weekday religious education. An article in a 1961 issue of the *Saints' Herald* encouraged jurisdictions to explore this opportunity for children and youth in school:

> Weekday religious education is coming of age. Although we, as yet, have paid little attention to this newcomer, it has shown a vigor and adaptability which commends it to the church.... While no branch should be pressured into weekday religious education before it is ready to assume such a responsibility, it does, nevertheless, seem apparent that the time for grasping hold of this new avenue of ministry is rapidly approaching, if not already here in many communities.[7]

Although for a number of reasons this opportunity did not seem to be extensively taken up, other ventures have been more fruitful. A resolution on International Christian Education presented to the 1974 World Conference and referred to the Council of Twelve brought a positive response. In a statement submitted to the First Presidency over the signature of Clifford Cole as president of the council, that body supported the intent of the resolution, encouraging the Department of Christian Education to find ways of responding. On the recommendation of the Twelve, such materials should include:

> Communication of the basic principles of Christian education to jurisdictional leaders, reflecting such considerations as distinctive cultural features, level of development of the respective missions, historical factors, and so forth, although the actual development of programs and production of materials shall be the primary responsibility of the national missions.[8]

The Basic Beliefs Committee

Yet another area in which Clifford's influence and leadership was clearly significant was in his leadership of the Basic Beliefs Committee from 1966 to 1970. For these significant years leading up to the publication of *Exploring the Faith,* he guided the group in an extremely exacting task, contributed several of the chapters accompanying the paragraph statements, and supervised the preparation of the manuscript for publication.

Clifford's report to the First Presidency and the World Conference pointed out that the beginning work of the committee had coincided quite closely with the introduction of the gospel in the framework of Oriental culture, highlighting the need to clarify its doctrinal message and to communicate sound faith in the larger world into which the church was moving. He described one of the major functions of the committee as the development of a "succinct statement of those beliefs which are most basic to the faith of the church":

> In the past, the closest thing we have had to such a statement has been the Epitome of Faith. This has been revised and reworded a number of times for use in setting forth some of the basic beliefs of the church. The committee has addressed itself to the task of developing such a statement. This project has consumed a major part of the time available to the committee. The study, discussion, and the struggle in framing the various parts of such a statement have been particularly rewarding to the members of the committee. However, one of the major concerns of the committee was its fear that any brief statement of the basic beliefs of the church might at some future time be regarded as a kind of creed, or binding statement, which might be used by some as a measure to prescribe what others should believe if they were to be considered in the faith.[9]

The Challenge of Education

A major statement on the role of education in the church was made by Clifford at the 1965 Kirtland Conference of High Priests, and printed in the December 1, 1965, issue of the *Saints' Herald.* The implication carried in the title was that, contrary to the opinion of some, the life of the mind and of the spirit were necessarily and closely connected:

> The Restoration movement as such has never believed in a separation of the physical and the spiritual things. Education has always officially been regarded as a necessary element in the discharge of one's stewardship. Nevertheless, individual members of the church have wrestled with the problems posed in educational pursuits, and, as a result, there have been individuals and groups with very distinct anti-educational feelings.... At our best, however, we do know that education needs the church and the church needs education.... It is when scholarship is linked with faith that men go to the threshold of the unknown and stand in awe as God takes the initiative to lead them through the doorway:[10]

As a leading voice in the development of new curriculum resources for the children and youth of the church, Clifford gave particular attention to the kind of climate that would best prepare such people to carry their faith into the future:

> First, [w]e can provide the kind of childhood climate and instruction which helps them evaluate honestly and make mature judgments. This is not well done in an extremely authoritarian church nor by authoritarian parents.... The tendency among the zealous is to think that the problems of those being lost to the faith can be solved if we drill the faith and convictions of the parents and church more indelibly into the minds of the youth.[11]

However, Clifford proposed, the outcome was generally far from what was hoped, and a brittle faith, based on insecure educational foundations, could prove inadequate to the challenges of the classroom. Such could result in disillusionment and resentment toward those who had hammered in an inadequate foundation:

> It is my candid opinion that we give our youth a much better basis for facing the modern world when we teach them the faith but in doing so face honestly with them the problems and uncertainties which this modern world poses to our beliefs and traditions. This is not out of harmony with the long-standing posture of the Restoration.... Any attempt to restrict or hamper an honest search for the truth is born out of fear that our own beliefs will not stand the searching analysis of investigation or that we shall be required to give up

our entrenched ideas and vested interests. The problem of the Pharisee is always with us and unfortunately in us.[12]

It might be said that faith without (educational) works is dead, to borrow a New Testament phrase. The wording might be different, but the underlying truth was sure. Accordingly, one of the major emphases of Clifford's apostolic leadership was to help elevate the theological understandings of the people through institutes and other settings for both leaders and people.

Education and Spiritual Maturity

Not so immediately obvious, yet still closely connected to the foregoing, was the concern to help encourage a spiritual depth among the Saints that would be exercised at a mature level and carry genuine evidence of hope:

> This was mostly done at reunions and conferences. I was concerned that our people came to understand that God is at work in all of our life's activities, leading and guiding us, and that He works in many ways. This was somewhat contrary to the feeling I found in the field that generally we as human beings were doing all of these everyday things alone and once in a while God kind of intervened and we had a spiritual experience in which a gift was given.... I was particularly concerned about that in terms of ministry at reunions. I found at that time that there were many people who felt that a reunion was a success if they could say we had a number of spiritual gifts there.... And I was pressing them to see that in our classes and in our preaching, in all of the reunion's activities, if there was a spiritual depth of understanding and love and warmth there, that God was in that too.[13]

Yet another concern had, in Clifford's experience, assumed major proportions. It was evident that during the struggles of the 1960s and 1970s there had been some attrition in the membership as a result of individuals becoming dissatisfied and leaving the church. These, he was disposed to believe, did not leave without voicing their dissatisfaction and drawing attention to the issues and people responsible. Yet he was convinced that at least an equal number, and possibly more, slipped away for the opposite reason:

> Actually the church had been losing the most forward-looking and especially those who had gone on in the field of education. As a result the church body as a whole, the more conservative element, looked at those more educated and more progressive persons with suspicion. I could name many personal friends who were among those. They tended after a while to feel shut out and disillusioned, and unwanted, and they silently drifted away.... And we lost, during that early period of time, great numbers of people who slipped away silently, but who could have been among the leaders of the church if we could have been able to hold them.[14]

In commenting further on the unrest of this time, and the charge that the loss was due to unwise church leadership, Clifford felt a substantial misunderstanding had arisen:

> The result was many people felt that we had been going along very well until leadership started making some changes and suddenly we got into all of this turbulence. What I am saying, then, is that I think we had been sustaining losses far greater, perhaps, by the people who had been silently slipping away from us before the 1960s. And to have waited longer would have meant that we would have just lost more and more of those people. I think it was time that we needed to take a new look at the church and re-evaluate our beliefs, our history, our mission, and I think the time was about up.[15]

To review Clifford's contribution in Christian education administration, in public ministry, through the many committees on which he served, and throughout his apostolic service is to perceive the extent to which his respect for and commitment to learning as a spiritual discipline was of major proportion. As always, underlying his pronounced advocacy of education, was the welfare of the church and its mission:

> An intelligent and dynamic people who would reach out to claim the loyalty of others in such a world as ours must look well to the foundation of their faith. Their undergirding faith must be able to stand when the clash of ideology against ideology is heard on every side.

The roots of their faith must be deeply grounded in truth which has stood the test of time. It is also important, however, that their faith be willing to accept and assimilate the expanding revelation of truth as it unfolds.[16]

Notes

1. *Exploring the Faith* (1970), Preface.
2. "Why They Loved Graceland: Four Graduate Farewells," in *Saints' Herald* (June 13, 1942): 13.
3. "On Being Guest Professor at Graceland," in *Saints Herald* (March 1983): 7, 10.
4. An Oral History Memoir, 40.
5. Ibid., 43.
6. Ibid., 37.
7. "The Church Looks at Weekday Religious Education," in *Saints' Herald* (June 19, 1961): 4–5.
8. "International Christian Education," in *Saints Herald* (January 1975): 6.
9. "Report of the Basic Beliefs Committee," in *Saints' Herald* (March 1970): 6.
10. "Education and Spiritual Power," in *Saints' Herald* (December 1, 1965): 16.
11. Ibid.
12. Ibid., 17.
13. An Oral History Memoir, 73.
14. Ibid., 261.
15. Ibid.
16. *Faith for New Frontiers*, 21.

CHAPTER 5
The Body of Christ

As suggested earlier, Clifford Cole's entry into the ranks of appointee ministers coincided closely with the commencement of a period, extending through the 1960s and 1970s, of unparalleled examination of the historical and theological foundations on which the church stood. It was perhaps inevitable that he should play a significant role in the process. Furthermore, it was of great value that his participation as a "calming and reasoned spirit" should be available for such a demanding task.

Foundation, Apostasy, and Restoration Revisited

Three substantial claims had been understood and proclaimed as the basis on which the church claimed the right to exist with unique, even exclusive authority. Briefly, these had to do with (1) the church established in purity, (2) an apostasy from the fullness and purity of that church, identifiable precisely in time, and (3) a historical restoration of the true church by divine initiative. The identification of a specific organizational structure, it was claimed, was mirrored in the Latter Day Saint structure as it emerged after 1830 and was a further witness to the authenticity of the church. The events of apostasy and restoration were fixed precisely in time to support the validity of these claims. However, as the church moved into the latter half of the twentieth century, serious questions were raised about the interpretation of the historical data and those prophetic statements on which these claims were based. Such concerns provided the impetus for the reappraisals of these years. The process itself, and some of the insights that issued from it, were extremely unsettling to many church members who felt that the very life of the church was being undermined. Those who possessed little or no knowledge of the way in which the church had met the challenge to change in earlier years looked on the current searching examination as totally unprecedented.

Clifford did not question the essential calling and mission of the church to represent Christ in the world:

> The conviction that God moved in the early experiences of the Latter Day Saint movement has given to the church a vital and dynamic testimony of (1) the active involvement of God in the world, and (2) the conviction that the church is of divine origin and is important to God as well as to humankind.[1]

However, given this basic affirmation, it was timely that three claims traditionally considered to be crucial to the validity of the movement should come under review. First, a more informed examination of the scriptures relating to the establishment of the New Testament church, as well as a more responsible acquaintance with other early Christian writings and history, yielded an alternative view of the nature and structure of the primitive church organization. Concerning the sense in which Jesus may have been said to establish the first-century church, Clifford wrote:

> It is our belief that Christ did establish the first century Christian church. This does not mean that Jesus fully organized and structured the church during the three years or so of his ministry here upon earth. Indeed, it is clear that he did not.... When we say that the church was established by Christ, we mean that Christ both through his physical presence and later through the Holy Spirit directed and empowered his disciples to establish his church upon earth. As the church grew, its organization and ministries became more complex as it moved to meet the needs of man, but the security of the church was not so much in its structure as in its divine leadership.... We ought not to read into the early Christian church the counterpart of our own organization and structure in any detailed way.[2]

Second, "apostasy" was more helpfully understood as a potentially ever-present condition of human beings, rather than as a precisely identified period of history based on questionable interpretation of prophecies from the books of Daniel and Revelation. Responsible historical examination simply did not support such a scheme:

> From the outset we need to recognize that this is not a black-and-white issue. It is not possible for us to say that one person or group is in apostasy and another is not. The basic problem of all of us is that apostasy is ever present with us.... Because of the sin within us, we are constantly in danger of bending the gospel to suit our own purposes rather than God's.[3]

Rather than viewing a certain period of history as suffering from the total withdrawal of the divine Presence, it would be more faithful to acknowledge the continuing presence of the Holy Spirit wherever the divine purpose was advanced:

> It would be wrong to say that the church at any time was totally bad or that it had no authority. In every age honest persons in the church have sought to serve God.... To some degree the community of believers has continued from the days of Christ to our present time. In fact, we could hardly see how there could be any church on earth at all if at any time after Christ's ascension the life and spirit of the Christian community had been totally blotted out. We recognize our indebtedness to the continuing Christian community through which the knowledge, spirit, and life of the incarnation have been preserved for us.[4]

Third, the Restoration movement initiated in 1830 could indeed invite our appreciation and commitment. Nevertheless, it should preferably be on more secure grounds than that at a certain prophetically predetermined point in history, the "true" form and faith of the church suddenly reappeared. In the same manner that apostasy was a continuing dimension of human experience, so restoration was a continuing characteristic of disciples under the impress of the Holy Spirit. The attempt to bring about "restoration" in the early nineteenth century was not unique to Latter Day Saints. The desire to bring back the primitive Jerusalem church "in spirit and in truth" constituted a major dimension in the revival, or "Great Awakening," of that period, and was a strong motivating factor in many religious groups that emerged at the time:

> In reality, however, the real genius of restoration in the founding experiences of the church through Joseph Smith was not so much in recapturing a church of the past as it was with renewed and vital contact with divinity.... Our biggest danger is that we assume that because we are the Church of Jesus Christ and have authority growing out of our experience with God, no other authority to represent God exists outside our own fellowship. This is not in harmony with our tradition, however. In the literature and tradition of the Reorganized Church of Jesus Christ the term when not used to identify a house of worship usually refers to the corporate organization and function of our particular Christian denomination. In the larger sense, however, Latter Day Saints have always believed in a broader usage of the term *church* to include those both living and dead who have truly responded under the Spirit of God to acknowledge Jesus Christ as their Lord.[5]

Clifford appreciated the efforts to examine history with the object of gaining a clearer view of the nature and message of the church. At the same time he believed this commitment to history and scripture had not always been undertaken from the worthiest of motives. Such motives were by no means unique to members of the early church; indeed they could be discerned in the writings of the New Testament records as these witnesses often turned to the Old Testament to prove that the prophecies recorded therein did indeed unerringly point to the Christ. At a churchwide college student conference at Graceland College in August–September 1967, he was asked to speak on the subject "The Doctrine of the Church." Reminding the gathering of the need for responsible scholarship and honesty in addressing this issue, he stated:

The Reorganized Church of Jesus Christ of Latter Day Saints was born in the midst of a great restoration movement. The church saw itself as being called to restore again the primitive order of things. Its attention was turned backward into history with an attempt to glean from its knowledge of the scriptures a clearer understanding of what the primitive church was and of the message which it taught. One cannot read the history of the past, however, without having a rather distinct feeling that many of the early founders of the church were not seeking so much to learn what the primitive church was from a study of history, but rather those early men felt that the true primitive church had been restored, and their study of history and the scriptures was an attempt to pick out those evidences which clearly justified the faith which had already been accepted and the image which the church already had about itself.[6]

The work of the Basic Beliefs Committee in the latter part of the 1960s reflected the felt need to clarify the faith of the church, to set forth its central affirmations, and to articulate more responsibly the scriptural and historical basis on which the church was founded. The statement accompanying the paragraph on the church was part of this search for greater validity in the positions taken by church members. While the fruits of such inquiry might at times have been disconcerting, and occasionally painful, the effort was critically important, and one to which Clifford brought his extensive background, shaped, as suggested earlier, "by study, and also by faith."

The Nature of the Church

Continuing a commitment to examine the role and mission of the church, leaders met in March 1977 to address the theme, "The Church and the Future." Almost a quarter-century earlier, in writing on this matter, Clifford had drawn attention to the tendency to impart a negative tone to the function of the church:

> This call of the Master to us is perhaps the most urgent need today, and it is to be deplored that we have often been content in the

past to think only in terms of obedience to the law. This has reflected itself in a negative attitude about the purpose of the church.

We sometimes make it appear as if the chief mission of the church is that of weeding out of men's lives the bad habits of tobacco, alcohol, swearing, thievery, and so on.

Most assuredly we are opposed to tobacco and alcohol and every other form of vice which ruins the health, destroys the character, and calluses the spiritual sensitiveness of men's souls. But it will be a sad day when the chief mission of the church in the eyes of its people is negative in its approach toward life. We shall not save ourselves by the things we don't do.[7]

Now he addressed the nature of the church in a significantly broader perspective. While acknowledging at least three major dimensions in the church's mission, the title of the paper "Meaning of the Church as Leaven," identified the major focus of the presentation. Before proceeding to this main emphasis, however, he lifted up the other two. The first he described as "helping people interpret the meaning and purpose of the world in which they live." This was a significant function, spoken or unspoken, in virtually everything that took place through ministry—in funeral ministry, the sacraments, and in most sermons.

> The ministry of interpretation and explanation of the universe in a way that makes sense, comforts, strengthens, and makes it possible for the human spirit to endure tragedy with dignity and look to the future with hope is an important function of the church.... It is, however, rather important that this function is inevitably related to the role of conservator of meaning and purpose, and therefore has a vested interest in the world in which that meaning makes sense. It tends to resist change and resent prophets.... In that spirit the church will sing with nostalgic unity "The Old, Old Path" and will be assured that this is indeed the good way.[8]

The second role of the church Clifford identified as "mediator." As such, the church provided "the means and the authority to relate persons of this world to the realm of the Spirit and the divine." Such a function filled, in his view, an amazing range of needs in society. Nevertheless, this too was not a function free of problems:

> This dimension of the church's mission is also a crucial one, and is seen by the majority of people as the avenue to divine favor in this life and the guarantor of "salvation" beyond that. The struggle that the church has always had with this dimension of its mission has been to keep the valid spiritual elements from degenerating into magic and to keep ritual and ordinances from becoming a substitute for genuine repentance.[9]

The third dimension was that of the prophetic. This was the dimension in which we sense the "oughtness" of life in the light of divine revelation. Here again, while the rhetoric gave prominence to the element of the prophetic—an open canon of scripture, the role of the prophet, the anticipation that the nations of the earth would come to Zion to learn of her ways—the reality left much to be desired:

> A thoughtful evaluation of our effectiveness as a prophetic voice in influencing the course of history is a good exercise in Christian humility. While the prophetic thrust of our movement is not wholly without effect, it is clear that the impact is far less than our aspirations. Furthermore, that impact has been primarily within our own institutional boundaries.... In all candor, however, our prophetic impotence may not have been so much in the softness of our voice as in the fact that we have largely been talking to ourselves about matters in which most of the world has little interest and because it is directed towards a world of the past rather than one of the present and future.[10]

The Great Divide

Clifford maintained that the world in the twentieth century had passed over a large divide, radically different from the world of the past characterized by separateness and isolation. The "new world" was characterized by
- the increase in speed and availability of travel,
- the onset of instantaneous communication,

- technical developments and industrialization,
- urbanization of the world's population centers, and
- interdependence of the modern world, rendering isolation obsolete,

all of which substantially effected the church's call to mission.

While some might mourn the loss of the past, wishing, among other things to preserve a view of Zion that presupposed the centrality of the "Center Place" and the preeminence of "the promised land," it was time to forge a new view of the present task and the future:

> Rather than being discouraged by crossing over the divide with the consequent changes we must face and the failures we sustain, it would be helpful to recognize the character of the new world we are entering. We have aspired to bring into being the kingdom of God. It is my firm belief that the interdependence and intensifying of human relations in a world which no one can escape is forcing us to deal with the questions of reconciliation, the recognition of all humans as of equal worth, the necessity to establish structures in society to facilitate personal fulfillment and justice, and the awareness that in this new world one group cannot long have blessings and privileges that are denied others.[11]

The Church as Leaven

Clifford expressed the opinion that in this emerging world, the church, with great humility and recognition of its limitations, might function more effectively as interpreter and mediator rather than as prophet:

> The mission into the world will primarily be as symbolized by Christ in the terms salt, light, and leaven. We have said for some time that we believe the Church should enter into the world as leaven but we have seldom pressed on the concept to see what it means in practical application.[12]

What strategies would best enable the church to fulfill its function as leaven? Clifford proposed that one of the most effective ways would be in the field of education. Acknowledging that institutions of education were an important area of influence in contemporary society, high-quality institutions sponsored by the church could exert a significant impact on attitudes and values. In the association of agencies of higher education the church-sponsored institutions, though small, could express their life in a wider environment. Further, Clifford believed, church-sponsored institutions of higher education might well serve as the most effective force for evangelism in the most responsible way.

Second, the church could encourage and inspire its members to "qualify for significant decision-making positions in government, business, health services, and so forth." Such members could make a decided contribution in terms of Christian values, deep spiritual reserves, and courage to stand for the right. In this arena the church might offer a significant ministry beyond its own membership boundaries:

> This is an opportunity to be a leavening influence in the lives of many who may not fully [accept] its lifestyle or desire for membership but who nevertheless recognize values of the ministry they receive and the fellowship they experience. We will need to welcome such with love, avoiding the temptation to pressure them to baptism. In this regard, I think it is presumptuous to tell persons in decision-making roles what their decisions should be.... To put it more bluntly, I doubt the fact that we are church members gives us any special insight into what President Carter should decide about any of the many decisions he should make.[13]

Third, the church should take its place in the larger Christian community. This was not to say that the church should become ecumenical in the strict sense of the term. Elsewhere he had written:

> We are not ecumenical in the sense of looking forward to the day when all Christian denominations will merge into one. Indeed, if this should happen it is my belief that it would be but a short time until another great reformation would need to take place. We are

ecumenical in the sense of cooperating with other church organizations for the common good that may be achieved by such efforts.[14]

While this was a role of great importance, and one that was readily within the reach of the church's ministry, full commitment was yet to be reached:

Unfortunately, our early beginnings were not conducive to cooperation with other Christian denominations. We are still so close to the days of interdenominational conflict that many of our members have a built-in rejection of materials written by any denomination other than our own, ecumenical cooperation is bad, and any affiliation with such a body as the National Council of Churches or the World Council of Churches is viewed as traitorous. If we are to see ourselves as leaven this ought to change.... I believe that the church brought to the world contributions of spiritual renewal, theological understandings and an impetus towards removing the barriers between the sacred and the secular which was and still is very important. But, like the yeast, it was never intended to be withheld from the loaf. Its contributions should be made in the larger Christian community.[15]

There were differences of opinion at that time [1977] on another front concerning the role of the church. Speaking to the college students gathered for the 1968 conference, Clifford had described the issue:

The extreme right wing of the church will say the purposes of the church are eternal and if we don't know them, then the church has drifted from the original faith; while the extreme left will say the suffering, injustice and estrangement of mankind cries out from every slum, disease-ridden community, war-twisted city and misguided mind. The world waits to be freed by those who bear the cross of humanity and this should be the church.[16]

Clifford acknowledged a measure of legitimacy both to the view identifying the chief role of the church to be the declaration of the gospel in the world, and the appeal for the church to be present wherever humanity suffers. Nevertheless, he believed significant qualifications needed to be attached to both. In the first place:

> It is the job of the church to make it possible for persons to meaningfully express the commitment of their lives and utilize the resources of their gifts in company with one another to achieve the purposes of God in the world. In the generation that is now rapidly passing, the achievement of this objective was set forth as the call to the church to "Evangelize the World." Unfortunately, time wears away the deeper implications of our statements and for many the phrase came to mean "getting people to be baptized." Certainly baptism is part of the act of commitment, but it has significance only when linked appropriately with the deeper meaning of evangelism.[17]

On the other hand, the pressure of those who would have reduced the church to the status of a social action group tended to overlook a basic element. Certainly the pains that afflicted human beings were real, and the causes aimed at removing them were virtually endless:

> Whether or not the church should address itself to those values is the basic question, but I must confess to you that I have a gnawing distrust of the interpretation given by many persons in our world today to the oft-quoted statement that "the church must let the world write its agendum." I think the quickest way for us to go into apostasy is for us to offer ourselves as a tool for every sincere movement to use for the accomplishment of its goals, even when those goals appear to be good. The surest way for us to be captured by the world is to allow ourselves to become vague about our central mission and therefore fall into the trap of either climbing on the bandwagon of some cause which appeals to us or becoming the antagonist of some movement or group that offends us.[18]

To this same major assembly of college students Clifford offered his judgment as to some general and eternal functions of the church, summarized as follows:

- to function as the custodian, preserver, mediator, and proclaimer of the gospel;
- to bring into being, preserve, and teach the scriptures;
- to provide the context in which members who are committed to Christ may bless one another through the exercise of their gifts and insights;

- to preserve the context in which our common worship may take place;
- to bring people into the presence of God through sacrament and ordinance;
- to strengthen us individually as we confront the evil that is in the world;
- to help us confront honestly the evil that is within us and become the victor over ourselves; and
- to organize and weld our gifts together to form the kingdom of God on earth.

The time was indeed portentous for those concerned to discern and put into effect the ministry of the church. Clifford concluded his presentation to the 1977 Joint Council seminar with an urgent appeal:

> It is time for the bonds of indecision to be loosed. Many have waited for that time and I am convinced that both the answers for those questions mentioned, and the struggle for those answers are an essential part of releasing the bonds of indecision. Furthermore, I believe that the problems which caused unrest during the past decade are essentially behind us, but our people will be disillusioned, and rightfully so, if we do not address the problems mentioned above in such a way that we can give aggressive and strong leadership into the future.[19]

Notes

1. "The Church," in *Exploring the Faith* (1987 edition), 144. The text accompanying the Basic Beliefs Committee's statement on the church was contributed by Clifford Cole. The 1987 edition was prepared by Alan D. Tyree.
2. *Exploring the Faith* (1970), 128–129, 131.
3. *Exploring the Faith* (1987), 147.
4. Ibid. (1987), 148.
5. Ibid., 131–133.
6. "The Doctrine of the Church," in "The Restoration in the Midst of Revolution," *University Bulletin* 20, nos. 2 and 3 (Winter 1968): 18.
7. "A Morality for Our Day," in *Saints' Herald* (December 6, 1954): 6.

8. "Meaning of the Church as Leaven," in a seminar of leaders (March 15, 1977), 2.
9. Ibid., 3.
10. Ibid., 4.
11. Ibid., 9–10.
12. Ibid., 11.
13. Ibid., 13.
14. "The Doctrine of the Church," 19.
15. "Meaning of the Church as Leaven," 15–16.
16. "The Doctrine of the Church," 12.
17. Ibid., 13.
18. Ibid., 12.
19. "Meaning of the Church as Leaven," 18.

CHAPTER 6

And Members in Particular

The range of Clifford Cole's concerns is indicated in the spectrum of age groups—from young children to senior adults—and the settings, including family, school, and congregation to which he directed attention in his writings. The concerns were essentially pragmatic: What kind of sensitivity and ministry is necessary to encourage the development of a "good" Latter Day Saint? The basic assumption, frequently stated, was that such a person would evidence a mature adjustment to the real world in which people lived out their lives, and bear a positive witness of the gospel in that world, with its conflicting demands and perplexities.

Underlying his writing, and frequently apparent, was Clifford's training, expertise, and commitment to the values of learning and faith. The writing, especially during the years when his assignment embodied a concern for children and youth, was deceptively simple. Nevertheless the principles were eminently sound, often ahead of the times, and always uncompromising in their invitation to effective discipleship.

Children and Youth

During his tenure in the Department of Religious Education, first as director of children's work and then as director of the department, Clifford lead the reappraisal of curriculum materials and programs for special groups, such as girls' work and Scouting. As stated earlier, he had expected to spend the entirety of his appointee life in this ministry and did not leave it readily. His interest in children's work was expressed in frequent contributions to *Guidelines to Leadership*, over a number of years the church's major publication to assist teachers and leaders in the various responsibilities of the congregations. He wrote about topics of immediate and practical concern to local leaders: the importance of visual aids and crafts for children's education, the significance of personal priesthood ministry to those children, and the resources available for prebaptismal preparation.[1]

Later, as a member of the Council of Twelve, he maintained these interests. When addressing the World-wide Women's Institute in April 1961, he described the importance of ministry to girls and promoted the value of the Oriole program. The church had been in the forefront of this program, prepared under the direction of the women's auxiliary in 1915 and endorsed at the general convention of that organization the same year. The need for such guidance, he felt, was necessary and timely:

> This is a confusing day for adults, but if it be confusing for adults how much more difficult it is for the young to keep their balance and to discern the right from the wrong. There is no resource of more value to us than our younger members, and in the feverish scramble of these days of living we must make certain that first, our vision is clear; and second, that we do everything necessary for the well-being and wholesome growth of our children.[2]

Still later, writing on behalf of the Council of Twelve, Clifford spoke to the matter of the sacrament of blessing of babies:

> In one sense the arrival of a baby in the world is not particularly unusual, but in another it is probably the most profound event of human experience.... As Latter Day Saints we have always treasured the experience of bringing our babies to the church and to God in the ordinance of blessing.... In recent years we may have become more casual about the blessing of babies than we ought.. . . While we are

talking about "Faith to Grow," perhaps one of the major emphases we need to rekindle is the blessing of little children and the responsibility which the church accepts with God for the creation of a new life.[3]

Clifford readily acknowledged the need for an effective outreach program to adults. However, perhaps the opportunities for which congregations wished were much closer than often realized. The ages between eight and twenty, he asserted, were a very significant and even decisive time for individuals to make many of life's most important decisions:

> This points up the very important responsibility which every congregation has for ministry to its children and youth.... For those who would like to see a more active missionary program in the branch, let the importance of this ministry to children and youth and the opportunities for effective evangelistic outreach be recognized as perhaps the major point where the church can extend its ministry most successfully and productively.[4]

The World of the Student

Equally strong was his concern for young students of high school and college age. The 1963 publication *The Revelation in Christ*, adapted for adult use, had originally been written as a senior high church school course for the previous year. Some time later, addressing the issue of "Education and Spiritual Power" at the high priests conference in 1965, by far the greater part of the presentation was devoted to the challenge of providing positive educational experiences for young people. A sound exposure to such opportunities was not without risk, but absolutely necessary if the church was to nurture mature and effective young people:

> Often we lose our own youth because we insist on determining what they should believe and do not trust them to use their own agency in the face of life's experiences. This approach has a great deal to say to church parents in the rearing of their children, but it also needs to

be kept in mind by those who prepare church school materials, select teachers, and minister to people. The agonizing struggle of the college student who finds his faith cracking up is often the result of unsound preparation for the experience of scholarship—and we should turn the light of blame on ourselves for this.[5]

No doubt informed by his own experience as a Graceland dean, Clifford strongly supported the value of continuing academic preparation in an environment of free inquiry. The attempt to be overprotective of young people, under the illusion that it would "save" them to the church, had proved to be both unsound and unproductive. We could best help our students, he proposed,

> by providing some institutions of higher education, particularly at the undergraduate level.... Our own institutions must not take from the student the privilege of honest investigation and analysis. There is no way to shield him from the struggles of confrontation with both fact and theory. Furthermore, we dare not do what some seem to recommend—that we so color the nature of the inquiry that the student is bound to have a negative reaction to what we dislike and a favorable response to the particular set of beliefs we espouse. We can, however, help him face his investigation in the presence of godly men and women who, having traveled the road ahead of him, can help by their presence to stabilize and sober him.... There is a vast crowd of both parents and students who are grateful for the fact that our church had institutions of higher education available to them.[6]

A decade later Clifford spoke to the issue of the situation of older youth in face of the gathering strength of the fundamentalist "awakening" in the United States. The impact of higher education, he acknowledged, had led many to expect that such young people would tend to be more liberal in their thinking and skeptical of tradition. The much-vaunted achievements of science had turned in on themselves and become harbingers of threat to the environment and even to life itself on the planet.

However, the assumption that young people would naturally approach the challenges of contemporary life with a faith that dared to explore new horizons was not verified in fact. It was true that the younger generation often seemed to exhibit lifestyles and habits abhorrent to the parents. However, such a judgment was not simply one-sided:

> They [young people] are appalled at the injustices of discrimination in regard to sex, race, or other identifiable classifications, the use of national wealth for military expenditures, the exhaustion of natural resources, and the dehumanizing effects of mass society which go unchallenged.
>
> Youth often feel that the adult world is full of hypocrisy. While on the one hand adults set high moral standards in respect to sex, family, honesty, and respect for other people, the adult society either secretly breaks those moral codes or through laws and accepted patterns of society disregards them without even feeling guilty about it.[7]

In the search for a simpler response to the demands of the current society, and in the search for a sense of worth, many young people were turning to the promises of fundamentalism, with its claim of complete and final answers to the problems of a very complex world:

> Many youth today are reacting against the permissive, affluent life that well-meaning parents—and sometimes uncaring parents—have created for their children. The simple black-and-white rigid rules of a fundamentalist faith provide the basis for developing an inner discipline, the feeling of success when the rules are kept, the security of knowing when success is being achieved, and the assurance of believing in a dependable future.[8]

Along with some possible values for older young people, the fundamentalist impulse carries some very real dangers. Apart from the negativism which tended to make its adherents discontented and judgmental, and the temptation toward a new kind of exclusivism and self-righteousness, fundamentalism could opt for simplicity rather than equipping persons to face the real and hard world. In light of these hard choices, Clifford expressed his hope for the young people who made up a significant proportion of the coming church:

> It is my sincere hope that they will neither retreat into the security of radical fundamentalism nor commit themselves too quickly to the adventure of theological innovation. If the lessons of history can be depended upon, we are greatly in need of a courageous generation which gives thoughtful and respectful consideration to the values which have grown out of the experiences of the past, but which also is so committed to the Lord Jesus Christ that it is willing to venture into the future with him knowing, as have those of all ages, that he calls people into a new life which can be lived only by new creatures in Christ.... We cannot achieve this by recapturing the past or by protecting ourselves from the pain of the future.... We are called to righteousness rather than self-righteousness, faith rather than fear, love rather than egotism, and intellectual understanding rather than irrationalism. Most of all we are called to be a people of God through whom his prophetic light can shine to the world.[9]

Women in Church and World

In the immediate aftermath of World War II and the years that followed, radical changes were taking place in the underlying structures of society and in the roles of women. While it would be another generation before women were admitted to the ranks of the ordained ministry of the church, changes of equal magnitude faced women who were sensitive to the demands and expectations of both church and the larger society. Such changes were of the same order that had won for women, against determined opposition, the right to vote less than two generations ago.

Clifford pointed to developments that had placed particular demands on women. U. S. society had rapidly moved from being predominantly rural to one in which four-fifths of the population lived in large towns or cities. For this and other reasons the fabric of home life had been transformed. In an earlier time, not so far distant

> Labor was organized so that the family got up together in the morning, ate their meals together, and did their work together. This was all considered part of the family relationship. In the very doing of the economic necessities, family unity was cemented.... Times are changing, however.... No longer does family unity automatically come as a by-product of earning an economic livelihood.[10]

In the earlier years of the communist regime in the USSR, various agencies were delegated the responsibility of providing care for children in order to free women for the work force. In a 1953 book, *The Recovery of Family Life*, Elton and Pauline Trueblood described this trend but also evaluated what had been happening in American society. Clifford made the following comments in 1955:

> In America we looked with horror on what we saw happening in Russia with its accompanying instability of family life. Now, however, we look back over our own history to see that we have delegated more and more responsibility to the school. The Truebloods concluded that we are voluntarily following the pattern which once we observed with such disdain.[11]

Others, however, pointed out that much of the discomfort and criticism aimed at "working women" arose not from some decline in values but from an inability to adapt readily to a changing society. Regardless of the particular reasons, the reality was that women, in particular, faced formidable challenges. Apart from potential difficulties that might arise when women earned an independent income, and the inevitable burden of duties borne by working wives, increased expectations descended on women who chose to stay at home:

> Let there be no confusion between the terms "housekeeping" and "homemaking." The real homemaker must be a financier, dealing with budgets, expense records, and getting the best values out of family expenditures. She must be a scientist, a dietitian, an efficiency expert, a psychologist, a social worker, and a diplomat.... These responsibilities of the home are not an interruption to her career. They are in very deed the career itself.[12]

But whether employed in the home or in the outside work force, women faced the complex and pressing demands of society in ways not universally recognized or understood. Although often experiencing great strains within herself, the mother might be expected to provide the peaceful, calming, disciplining, and stabilizing presence that many males presumed—even demanded—as a refuge from the pressures of the world of work:

> Today's women have difficulty defining and clarifying their areas of responsibility. They find themselves being pulled by the demands of organizations, community groups, and family responsibilities which seem to be timed on a split-second schedule. How can one stretch one's time to do all the commendable and important things which she is asked to do and which she wants to do?... Those who talk about the leisure which our scientific discoveries and time-saving devices have supposedly made for us just haven't faced the demands placed upon both men and women who want to be active in the church and community today.[13]

While admitting that there are no simple answers to the many and various demands facing the "modern" woman, Clifford nevertheless pointed to the scriptures as a major resource for women to be engaged in a lifestyle that was both significant and productive:

> Where shall the woman of today find the resources to face life and live it triumphantly? While the problems are many, certainly the resources are no less abundant, and this should also encourage us. Among the greatest of these resources are the scriptures.... Ofttimes, what we really find in the scriptures is not some means to change the outward situation that we believe to be unbearable but rather a new inner power and direction which lifts us above the situation and helps us to see it and ourselves in a new light. The solution, then, becomes one of transcending the problems and redirecting our lives...the basic resource we need is within.[14]

Marriage and Family

Although Clifford recognized that different lifestyles

would be represented in the church membership, it was clear that all persons had been part of a family, and that many were currently part of a family structure in a marriage that was of long standing or that was in the early stages. He cited church membership records that appeared to indicate a large number of single persons, who needed specialized ministry. At the same time, the church was concerned about marriage as one of the most significant settings for nurture of the young and as a place for expressing the Christ-centered witness. The incidence of divorce, signifying the failure of the commitments made in marriage to prove effective, was a source of concern to the church leadership:

> One of the growing problems of our day and a symptom of our culture is the unwillingness of many people to make long-range commitments in their lives. We are approaching a crisis in the alienation of men and women from the Spirit of God.... The rising divorce rates throughout the world represent merely the outward evidence of a vast alienation which precedes the final act of divorce. Even within our own faith the divorce rate is notably higher than a generation ago and probably only slightly better than in the world around us.[15]

A major problem, in Clifford's view, was the widespread failure to achieve and maintain reconciliation, whether on an interpersonal or national level. The consequences of our failure had, in his opinion, "become ghastly." Yet it was only the larger repercussions, at a national or international level, that could bring us to the brink of disaster. The failure to be reconciled was equally, and even intimately, associated with breakdown in the home:

> For many of us the need for reconciliation exists most acutely within the family. For many the difficulty of reconciling differences between husband and wife or between child and parent leads to unhappiness and warped personalities. Conflict in the home is the rule rather than the exception.... How shall we meet the intimate prob-

lems faced in our homes except it shall be through the power of God which softens our hearts? We have need to be reconciled both with one another and with Him.[16]

Clifford explored another element of effective family life in the publication *Celebrating Together in Our Families*. Family celebrations fostered the common bond among families, provided special times of enjoyment, and preserved the spirit of commemoration. Whether such celebrations had to do with the family's story, with national days, or with the spirit of remembering in the church, people were the victims of their own amnesia when they used such times only for the escapism or enjoyment of the moment. The recognition and celebration of our past provides a foundation for meaningful participation in the present and genuine hope for the future.

For a wide range of reasons, then, the family provided the environment and motivation for healthy, innovative, and faithful growth. For those individuals who chose marriage as the basic relationship for their life's experience, the home became a vital center of wisdom and unity:

> The choices which we make in the development of our families are tremendously important. The consideration of marriage is significant and important to the church, for through our homes there must go out the most effective testimony of the new life which we have found in Christ. In Zionic homes, faith may be shared by children and parents alike, that their dedication to God may unify them in a combined witness to the community and to the world.[17]

Notes

1. Refer to the Bibliography for articles appearing in *Guidelines to Leadership*.
2. "Ministry to Girls in a Changing World," in *Priesthood and Leaders Journal* 1, no. 9 (November 1961): 36.
3. "Our Children," in *Saints Herald* (October 1979): 32.
4. "Ministry to the Under 20's," in *Saints Herald* (September 1975): 6.

5. "Education and Spiritual Power," in *Saints' Herald* (December 1, 1965): 17.
6. Ibid.
7. "Theological Issues Confronting Older Youth Today," in *Saints Herald* (September 1976): 17.
8. Ibid., 18.
9. Ibid.
10. *Working Together in Our Families* (Department of Women, 1955), 7.
11. Ibid., 18–19.
12. Ibid., 24.
13. *Modern Women in a Modern World* (written for the Department of Women, 1965), 16.
14. Ibid., 18–19.
15. "The Church Is Interested in Marriage," in *Saints' Herald* (November 1969): 10.
16. Source unknown.
17. "Women in a Witnessing Fellowship," in *Saints' Herald* (December 22, 1958): 13.

CHAPTER 7
Into All the World

As might be expected from a person who served many years as the presiding officer of the church's chief missionary quorum, Clifford Cole's predominant theme through speaking and writing had to do with the outreach of the church in mission. In virtually every setting available, Clifford endeavored to challenge church members to come to an understanding of the nature of this mission and to perceive it, not as one of the optional avenues of ministry open to the church, but as the fundamental and total reason for its existence. His writings on this theme include World Conference sermons (which shall be considered separately), Joint Council seminars, the Theology Commission, gatherings of students and women, and other particular gatherings such as high priests, and stake and region leaders.

Clifford believed it was critical to understand evangelism as the "central pivot of the church around which all other issues revolve and from which they take their meaning."[1] This was important both for the manner in which the church shaped its own inner life, and also for the way it related to the world around it; and in truth these were not two separate phases of the church's existence but necessarily one. Citing a description of evangelism given by the Madras Foreign Mission Council, Clifford offered a blunt appraisal:

> Although we make statements like this from time to time, it is very easy for us to give lip service but then go on to conducting business as usual by quite different standards and for quite different purposes. Nevertheless, what we do about evangelism is crucial to the question of whether or not we are the Church of Jesus Christ. A school

which does not engage in education can hardly call itself a school...a church which does not "present Jesus Christ to the world in the power of the Holy Spirit that men shall come to put their trust in God through Him, accept him...and serve him as their Lord in the fellowship of the church" cannot hold a valid claim to be the Church of Jesus Christ.[2]

Speaking to a gathering of high priests and spouses in 1971, Clifford defined mission as:

[T]hat framework of faith or belief that impels the church to reproduce in the midst of society the patterns of life implied in the life of Christ and to work for the adoption of those patterns in such a way that the kingdoms of this world may literally become the kingdoms of our God and his Christ. Such a theology calls us to be the disciples of Christ participating with him in his mission.... Perhaps one of the most penetrating descriptions [of this mission] given by Christ was: "The Spirit of the Lord is upon me, because he hath anointed me to preach the gospel to the poor, he hath sent me to heal the broken-hearted, to preach deliverance to the captives, and the recovering of sight to the blind; to set at liberty them that are bruised; to preach the acceptable year of the Lord." The theology of mission is this theology of doing the work of God in the world because we are committed to the fact that it is his world and he loves it.[3]

Nevertheless, while expressing in the same address the belief that the church had been more consciously committed to mission than most Christian bodies, he also voiced the belief that the path to a sounder understanding and practice of evangelism had not come easily. It could not properly be denied that the Restoration movement, entering the scene in the early years of the nineteenth century, was relevant to its times and to the religious, social, and political issues of the day. This appraisal of the early church has been pointed out by one of the major sociologists of religion in the United States in his study of the Latter Day Saints.[4] The church was established with a sure sense of the continuing revelation of God as it addressed its mission, and with a strong commitment to establishing "the cause of Zion" in the midst of the nations. In this sense it was surely among the most "worldly" of institutions.

However, circumstances over which the members of the church had little control produced an unfortunate effect:

> The Restoration came forth to proclaim this universal gospel. Perhaps it is because the Restoration was immediately attacked by other religious organizations that we in times past have emphasized so strongly those beliefs which distinguish the Restoration from other denominations.... We felt it necessary to meet the attacks which were made upon us by enemies who tried to destroy the Restoration movement.... We dare not, however, allow ourselves the luxury of spending much time in justifying ourselves or defending the gospel. This inevitably turns our attention upon ourselves and upon our church, rather than upon Christ and his church.[5]

It was some time before the impact of these early experiences, and the church's response to them, became distressingly evident. Under the perceived imperative to "defend" the church, major time and energy was directed toward our overidentification with the Old Testament images of "Israel" (as in the claim to be "Latter Day Israel"), interpretations of scripture and history that were more directly concerned with self-defense than in outwardly directed mission, and in claims to exclusive authority, doctrine, and structure. It was as if the church had taken steps to "circle the wagons" to defend itself against the "outside" world, all too frequently identified as "gentiles":

> The fact that the church has from time to time slid back into the pit from which it sought to lead the world, is not surprising. Seldom even in the work of God are leaps of progress made without periods of retrogression or some carry over from the social and spiritual distortions out of which it came....We are now in an interesting and crucial time in the history of the church. We have an immediate history of introversion. We have been far more preoccupied with ourselves than we ought to have been. This has affected our evangelism and yet many of us are crying from the housetops answers to questions few people are asking.[6]

The Changing Face of Evangelism

What this meant was that the church had allowed itself to be diverted from its calling to expend energy, resources, and personnel in an introverted mode. This not only affected the message the church presented to the world but tended to undermine the unity of the body:

> It became ever more clear as we approached the decade of the 1960s that we had turned in upon ourselves and in doing so were losing a sense of mission to the world. We were increasingly bogging down in our internal dissensions.... Furthermore there was a belief held by many of the church leaders that the missionary message and approach we had all inherited from the past had lost the relevance it once held.... Others, particularly the younger members, were often heard to say, "I am really not interested in proof that the Reorganized Church of Jesus Christ of Latter Day Saints is the true church; I want to know if this church has anything to help me with the major problems of my life, or anything that speaks significantly to the issues that are confronting our world."[7]

There were members who saw the developments that generally came to a head in the 1950s and marked the strains of the two decades that followed as cause for mourning and evidence that the church was descending into apostasy. There were others who saw these same circumstances as evidence of the church responding, under the Spirit of God, to a faithful call to mission. Clifford Cole shared this belief and may be said to be one of those who not only saw a different future for the church, but gave significant leadership in the response to that vision:

> I thank God that there has always been those forces within the church and that prophetic leadership that has led us on and out of the pit. By this I do not imply that we are without error or above confusion, but I do have a profound faith that the tradition from which we come and the Holy Spirit which guides us will constantly redirect us into God's mission and restore us as his people to the best we know and to our commitment to him.[8]

Speaking at the Conference of High Priests and Seventies in 1971, Clifford drew attention to the massive changes that had taken place in a relatively short time, arising from technological, social, and cultural developments. "It would be unrealistic," he asserted, "to presume that any church could survive from 1830 to 1971 without a great deal of inner turmoil." The need for an earnest reassessment of our mission, including a candid reappraisal of the message and methods of evangelism had been evident for some time but had emerged as particularly stressful, though necessary, during the previous decade. Adjustments had been called for in priorities and objectives, church organization, perceptions of the Zionic task, relationships between the World Church and local jurisdictions, and even in some theological points of view:

> In the midst of these changes many people feel threatened and often bitterly resent having the foundations upon which their lives are based questioned and sometimes reordered by persons over whom they have no control.... Many feel that they have been dragged against their will from a life which seemed stable into a world which they did not make, based on values which they do not like. The church is caught squarely in the midst of this, and while we have during the last few years experienced considerable turbulence, I believe we have come through this period with remarkable ease when we consider the distance we have traveled in so short a time. Furthermore, I am tremendously encouraged by the vitality and enthusiasm of the members as they confront the mission of the church. They are responding in a devoted and sacrificial way.[9]

The forward movement of the church to which Clifford had been referring was influenced by a number of factors:
- a new concern about mission emerged in the church;
- the work began opening in new areas, predominantly in non-Christian cultures;
- the Joint Council continued to move toward unity, with respect both to theology and strategy for addressing the mission;

- the Department of Christian Education began preparing a new graded curriculum; and
- financial stringencies prompted the need for new strategies in administration and evangelism.[10]

The Church Expands Its Mission

In the midst of these developments an event took place that was to have repercussions far beyond the immediate occurrence, and possibly unforeseen at the time. The First Presidency commissioned two apostles to visit the Orient to gauge the prospects of opening a mission there, following up on initial contacts that had been made. Shortly thereafter Apostle Charles Neff was assigned to take up residence in the Orient, and he was soon joined by other appointee families. The effect of movement into a non-Christian culture, as described by Clifford, was remarkable and highly significant for the growth of the church's mission. This unprecedented movement confronted the church with the inadequacy of a missionary message depending on "distinctives" in a culture where only 3 percent of the population was Christian. The church was inevitably thrust into closer and more sympathetic relationships with other Christian denominations. Equally important, this development prompted a deeper appreciation of the necessity and values of indigenization, accompanied by the need to decentralize the administration of the church.[11]

The implications of this development will be explored more fully in the next chapter. Suffice it to say here that it would be difficult to find a single aspect of the church's life that was untouched by the repercussions of this particular event.

However, there were missional tasks to be confronted, not only in the new fields being opened up, but throughout the entire church. A renewed call to evangelism could not be issued on the more traditional grounds but would need to grow out of a clearer vision of the role and mission of the church in the world. Clifford had observed a growing willingness on the part of many church members to be involved in a significant and relevant ministry to enable missionary expansion:

> This will help many who want to work in a significant way to be involved in the church's mission. This will free us to new action in which persons may find a genuine sense of worth in being involved in the mission and work of the church. This will draw many to the church who want to be part of a cause that gives worth and meaning to their lives. Many will unite with the church when they find it offering them the opportunity to be persons of worth.[12]

A growing sense of the church's mission inspired a deeper awareness of and sensitivity to those in need, who years later would come to be known as "the bruised and brokenhearted." Nurtured in part by the contact with other cultures in which need was a daily problem, church members began to reach out to others in their own culture:

> This is seen in the amazing response of the church's membership to help both with money and time to minister to people in the newer missions abroad. It is seen in the greater interest of reaching out to the American Indian, ethnic groups of the inner city, and others who were largely ignored for many years. It is seen by the involvement of our members in neighborhood councils and community activities for the betterment of others.[13]

Members in the Western nations tended to experience a more affluent lifestyle than many whom they were discovering as needing the ministries of the church. Where once such affluence might have been seen as a sign of divine favor and preference, it was more and more understood as a resource for reaching out in the spirit of Christ. This, too, constituted a challenge to church members. Very early in his assignment as a World Church minister Clifford had pointed to this new dimension of ministry:

We Americans prefer to go first class when we travel through a nation. We need to live with the common people where our hearts ache amid the suffering of others. We must be discontented and dissatisfied to live a life of ease while most of the world is sick, poverty stricken, and hungry...

Today the church needs people who sense the yearning within the heart of God for those borne down by ignorance, superstition, poverty and disease and—sensing that need—feel themselves called to a divine partnership in ministry to those who need them.... Men and women must respond who are so concerned that they are willing to share the life of those in other lands and become identified with them.[14]

The Witnessing Congregation

It was readily recognized that, except in special circumstances, the congregations of the church are the front lines for evangelism. If the local congregation is not evangelistic in outlook and activity, then it is difficult to see how the mission of the church could be proclaimed and embodied in that place. Writing on behalf of the Council of Twelve in 1970, Clifford reminded the members that they confronted the mission with a new sense of freedom, which was at once a blessing and a challenge:

We have opened missions in non-Christian lands. We have opened the door to becoming a world church. We have been confronted by a theological revolution. This means, essentially, that we have grown to the place where we no longer feel we are required to justify or prove the viability of our existence. We do exist. We are a great church. We do not have to defend ourselves. We are, however, called to mission. We are called to accomplish the work of Jesus Christ in the world and every year, in every congregation, we ought to ask, "What would Jesus Christ have us do in this community this year?"[15]

In this respect, however, despite the favorable environment in which the church found itself and the profession of mission that might be proclaimed, congregations did not automatically make the necessary adjustments in priorities, programs, and assignment of personnel to address the mission:

> A branch doesn't coast into evangelism. The inertia of the immediate and pressing needs of the congregation always resists the pull toward missionary work. The budget must be raised and buildings constructed or repaired. Sermons must be preached, services planned, records kept, and activities conducted. We turn our attention in upon ourselves. Indeed, if the church members are not kept interested, organized, and active, the consequences often bring embarrassment to the church, and the branch is weakened. Although our own desires clamor for attention, we seldom really feel the reproach of the unbaptized.[16]

Notwithstanding these temptations, the fellowship of the Saints gathered in congregational life was a potentially powerful source of ministry for those outside the fellowship. The spirit and power of that fellowship was not only to be observed but experienced. "It is experienced," wrote Clifford, "as an unfeigned love from the genuinely saintly concern that reaches out and draws persons into the fellowship." In a time when the close relationships of an earlier period appeared to be lost in the impersonal and complex life of contemporary societies, there were many who yearned for some sense of stability to give their lives a grounding. In the warmth of a fellowship that people might encounter in the congregation, and in the spirit of worship by which they could become aware of a personal God at work in their lives, people could experience a genuinely sustaining and empowering love:

> That kind of love is not easy to come by. It is the love of God which is akin to his grace, but there is no other force which heals the distorted, sin sick, and defensive souls and hearts of persons. I am convinced that more people are decisively influenced to say 'yes' to Christ and the church from the experience of acceptance and love experienced in the fellowship of the Saints than by any other one cause. I am convinced that any congregation that genuinely loves and is concerned about a specific person will find a way to draw him into the fellowship.[17]

While the power of fellowship is indispensable to evangelistic outreach and is at the very heart of the message, that message should always be intellectually honest and free of manipulation. Positive feelings and sincerity do not dismiss the obligations of integrity:

> Whatever else we may say about methods of evangelism we can never get away from the fact that our message must be true. The church must be honest and open. It cannot command the respect of persons who are seeking truth unless the church is prepared to give open and honest consideration to the issues which are significant to the world. Quotations of scripture, laments for a past generation, or simplistic answers will not help evangelism in our time. There is need for frank and unbiased consideration of the issues which are important to people's lives. The church should not feel threatened to engage in such exploration, for inasmuch as the church is soundly based, it need not fear the test of examining its own foundations and patterns of life.[18]

A Place for the Institution

Clifford was witness to the upheavals of the times which brought into question virtually all authorities, structures, and institutions, whether societal or ecclesiastical. Such were considered to inhibit the free movement of the creative impulse, or preserve traditions at the expense of real reform. The RLDS Church did not escape this kind of judgment:

> During the last few years there have been some who belittle the organized church as if its institutionalization was a detriment to God's purposes. Let it be clear that persons who have paid a great price to establish and maintain an institution always face the danger of idolizing the structure that they have established. The fact that such dangers are always present in no way invalidates the necessity for institutions. All human relationships require some kind of social patterns and some institutionalization. God has purposed to develop human personality not in some isolation apart from society, but in the midst of the community. The church is the community of those who are committed to Christ and are struggling in the midst of soci-

ety to fulfill the purposes of God.... As much as we have been embarrassed to speak of the church as essential to salvation, there is no way for persons to become reborn except in the midst of the reborn community.[19]

Clifford expressed great confidence, not so much in the church as such, as in the God whose presence by the Holy Spirit magnified the gifts of those who composed the fellowship to fulfill the divine purpose. He had a profound insight into the historical background out of which the church had arisen, and a close-hand engagement with the tensions and struggles that had been so much a part of the middle years of the century. His faith in the advancement of the church's mission in the years to come was overwhelmingly strong:

> In a sense evangelism is an endeavor of romance. It involves the love of God reaching out to win persons to him, but it also involves the love of the church who is the body of Christ reaching out with Godly love to win others into the fellowship. The love of God will be experienced as it is expressed in the fellowship of the church which cares for mankind. No lover is without the necessary imagination to find ways to meet and draw his beloved into association, but he must be worthy of that association. In a very real sense I am convinced that God will give us success in evangelism as we are worthy of success. I believe the great struggle within the church to find the mission God is calling us to will help open a new era of vital and fruitful growth in which many will be won to the faith.[20]

Notes

1. From an unpublished manuscript, "The Nature of Evangelism" (May 1974), 1.
2. Ibid.
3. "The Theology of Mission," an address to high priests and spouses (March 20, 1971), 1.
4. Whitney R. Cross, *The Burned-Over District* (New York: Harper and Row, 1950), 145–146.
5. "The Restoration Is Universal," in *Saints' Herald* (November 1, 1962): 9.
6. "The Theology of Mission," 6.

7. "The World Church: Our Mission in the 1980's," in *Commission* (September 1979): 42.
8. "The Theology of Mission," 6.
9. "Theological Perspectives of World Mission," in *Saints' Herald* (July 1971): 10–11.
10. "The Evolution of Evangelism in the 60's and 70's," a paper prepared for the Evangelism Commission (September 16, 1980), 5–10.
11. "The World Church: Our Mission in the 1980's," 42–43.
12. Ibid., 44.
13. Ibid., 43.
14. "A Morality for Our Day," in *Saints' Herald* (December 6, 1954): 6.
15. "The 1970's: A Decade of Promise," in *Saints' Herald* (February 1970): 7.
16. "The Branch Looks at Its Calling," in *Saints' Herald* (November 1, 1963): 10.
17. "The Nature of Evangelism," 9.
18. "Foundations for Contemporary Evangelism" (n.d.), 13.
19. Ibid., 4–5.
20. Ibid., 14.

CHAPTER 8

From Isles and Continents Afar

In an earlier chapter, the extension of the church into the Orient was described by Clifford as the crossing of a divide. Prior to this time the church had been established, with varying degrees of success, in Christianized Western nations. The single non-Western culture where the church had been present for more than a century was French Polynesia. However, even in this instance, the predominant environment and values were Christian. With the movement of the church into the Orient and other non-Christian cultures during the next decade, a great divide was indeed crossed. No aspect of the church's experience was untouched by this development.

A simple listing of the countries the church entered demonstrates the extent of the change. Although in some cases members had been baptized in these places, formal organization presumed increased growth that would require a greater investment of church resources, both in terms of finances and personnel. In considering this list, it gives cause for both interest and wonder that in some cases the initiative lay not with representatives of the church but with inquiring individuals from outside the fellowship. In the first decade after 1960 the following missions were established:

1960	Japan	1968	New Caledonia
1960	Korea	1968	Haiti
1961	China (Taiwan)	1969	Fiji
1964	Mexico	1970	Argentina

1965   Peru
1965   Brazil
1966   Nigeria
1966   India
1966   Philippines

1972   Honduras
In 1970, India Church
divided into:
    South India
    East India

To See with New Eyes

Although from the very beginning of the Christian community disciples had professed a commission to go and "make disciples of all nations" (Matthew 28:19 NRSV), missionaries had interpreted this command as an obligation to draw converts out of a fallen world into the protection of the church. "Otherworldliness" was considered a virtue to be energetically sought after:

> The temptations to self-centeredness have always plagued the church, and the history of the church shows all too well that it has from time to time regressed into exclusivism looking out at the world as an enemy and viewing the so-called culture of the world as evil. In fact it has become common for the term "world" or "Babylon" to be used to designate that evil society from which the followers of Christ are rescued. This idea became well established in the Middle Ages. Sacrificing the things of the world was essential to becoming holy.... The centripetal force of inward concern led religious people away from a concern for mission to a primary concern about personal salvation.[1]

In essence, a profound and even traumatic experience preserved in the New Testament had been submerged in the concern for self-preservation, as Christians "saw their vocation as requiring them to keep the pollution of the world out."[2] Although frequently cited, and indeed lifted up as describing a crucial turning point in Peter's experience, the implications were largely ignored:

> Peter was informed, "What God has cleansed, make thou not common" (Acts 10:15).... The implication of Peter's experience was that not only foods and material things were not evil but other nations of people were God's concern.... Peter was led into such a traumatic

experience that he was impelled to exclaim, "Of a truth, I perceive that God is no respecter of persons, but in every nation he that feareth him, and worketh righteousness, is accepted with him" (Acts 10:34–35).... In Christ, nothing is unclean of itself; barriers separating people of differing race and nationality and sex and class are broken down.[3]

Although, in Clifford's opinion, the Restoration movement had suffered from this same temptation to inward piety from time to time, the fundamental sense of mission, often expressed as "the cause of Zion," had helped preserve an awareness of the church's call to reach out beyond its own boundaries.

Despite this, the initial movement of the church into nations and cultures other than those that were predominantly Christian in their broad range of values confronted leaders and members with unexpected challenges. Before 1960 the basic faith structures of those nations where the church was established were shared by the Reorganized Church to the extent that the major focus of the missionary message centered on "those concepts which are more peripheral to the central Christian faith but which we put into a category called distinctives."[4] This situation underwent serious reexamination in the 1960s following the visit of two apostles to the Orient.

When we go as a church into the non-Christian world we are not dealing in its missionary witness with peripheral issues. We are challenging the basic faith structure that holds the society together. We should expect when we do this that the results will constitute a major confrontation. There is at the very least a fundamental confrontation with culture. We tend to dissolve and suspend the gospel in large quantities of Christian culture until neither we nor they know how much of the cultural vehicle is essential to the active Christian ingredient.[5]

When the Gospel Encounters Culture

The principles of Christian faith were not merely a series of teachings that could be overlaid on an existing culture, requiring merely that some peripheral patterns of behavior should supplement the regular way in which people understood and conducted their lives. Although such a confrontation might come to be largely overlooked and ignored in the so-called "Christian" countries, a far more profound challenge could not be ignored as the church extended its missionary presence:

> Culture may be defined as that whole complex of customs, morals, knowledge, beliefs, art, and other material and nonmaterial developments acquired by persons as members of a society.... Since culture is the means through which each society attempts to meet human need it should be considered good or bad in the degree to which it is able to meet both the innate human needs and those which the culture creates for all of the people.[6]

Some challenges became apparent immediately:

> The founding experiences of the church pointed to the Book of Mormon with its message of God's blessings on the land of Joseph. The Center Place in Missouri, the gathering of the Saints to Zion, and the establishment of the New Jerusalem all focused attention on America. People in any part of the church developed an allegiance to this new land as their anticipated home so that even if their migration was delayed they looked forward to the time when they would be gathered in. They became marginal members of their own culture and in a sense strangers in the land of their birth.[7]

But the situation had changed drastically from the earlier years of the church, when migration to the United States was considered highly desirable. In the more developed nations, the appeal of a higher standard of living in the United States, along with theological understandings about Zion, had encouraged such migration.

However, the passage of time had brought about significant changes in this situation. Increased living standards in other Western nations had diminished the desire of many members to leave their homeland for residence in the United States, while a growing sense of nationalism among both developed nations and those in the early states of independence had prompted citizens to see their future being worked out in their own homelands. Interpretations that had supported tendencies toward migration were applicable in a period of history and a cultural setting that no longer existed. The need to rethink the Zionic call would take place in light of significant questions, including

> [T]he questions raised by our newly formed missions throughout the world and the growing reluctance of persons in the nations of the earth to move to the United States. It will be intensified by the growing sense of nationalism and the feeling of the people of other nations that their full allegiance should be to their own nation and culture.... Persons in our missions abroad feel their own land is sacred and as divinely created and endowed as any other. In fact, when we speak of "missions abroad" they want to know "abroad" from what. The increasing limitations placed by immigration laws do and will limit the number of people who can come to a Zion which is exclusively American even if they wanted to.[8]

To accept the reality of this situation meant that the future of the church in each culture would, as quickly as possible, rest with the indigenous members of the church in that location. This fact carried implications both for the allocation of funds and the assignment of personnel, which in turn had a bearing on the distribution of responsibility:

> If the church in other nations is to be freed from the heavy hand of American domination the national churches must develop the resources to support themselves. These administrative units must provide the economic resources, manpower, leadership, confidence, and morale to stand on their own feet, and be the church where they are located.... This means that we must stop setting up facilities and programs which are artificial to the culture and unsupportable through the resources of the indigenous church.... To fail in this is to keep these national missions dependent on the world church with headquarters in the United States.[9]

The Heart of the Gospel

Accompanying this need was one of equal importance, and possibly demanding an even greater change of perspective by the "domestic" church:

> With the growing willingness to accept responsibility, there must be freedom of autonomy given. The church in each nation needs to hold its property, maintain its juridical person, and determine its program within its own national structure. As far as I am aware, no Christian denomination has ever grown to be very significant in any country where this kind of autonomy has been denied....Some will say, "What, then, holds the church together?" To this I must reply that it is held together by its commitment and its allegiance to the world church, not by having its decisions made in the Joint Council or its property held in the name of the World Church.[10]

What impact did these understandings carry for the substance of the message, or the gospel, as the church moved into other cultures, especially into non-Christian cultures? One byproduct, as it were, of the direction the church felt "driven" to move by the demands of integrity was a polarization that arose because some members regretted the decreasing emphasis on our distinctives. However, unexpected blessings came with the decision:

> Our differences with other Christian denominations were of little interest to the non-Christians we were trying to convert. They wanted to know essentially what Christianity teaches. We were forced to give a new consideration to the question, "What is essential to our faith?" Strangely enough, when we seriously came to grips with this, we found that the most important basics of our faith were shared by many other Christian denominations. This did not make these basics any less important, and when we began exploring their meaning without regard to whether or not other persons believed them, we found ourselves greatly strengthened in our own faith. When we began preaching, writing, and teaching the full range of the gospel of Jesus Christ, it was almost as if a window had been opened letting in light and fresh air.[11]

This highlighted the need, in Clifford's view, to determine more precisely "what it is about the church that is true all the time everywhere," to identify and proclaim "the universal truths of the gospel."[12] As leaders and members began to mine the resources of the faith they developed a new appreciation for the richness of the church's message. They also came to understand that the RLDS Church possessed some valuable insights into a number of principles that were, in fact, a unique offering to the larger Christian world, insights that had been accepted almost without thought and often taken for granted by the Saints.

A New Appreciation for Culture

Perhaps the most difficult decisions, and the attitudes supporting those decisions, rested in the ability to express a genuine confidence in the power of the gospel to bear its fruit in the midst of, and sometimes despite the cultures where it took root:

> In a very real sense this has created problems of adjustment much greater than we anticipated. It has forced us to look at the church through the eyes of people living in other cultures, in lands far from America and among races that have not been commonly found within our membership. Concepts which were once glibly held about such matters as Zion, Joseph's land, the curse of the Lamanites, and the relationship of our church movement to the political system and social customs have had to be reexamined. The problems arising from our work among the diverse cultures of our missions have made some wish that we had never ventured so far abroad.[13]

Nevertheless, the outreach of the church obliged scrutiny not only of the place of "Joseph's land" in its worldwide mission, but called for a new appreciation of other cultures:

> A further serious matter requiring adjustments in our consideration has to do with our continued delusion that we are in some way carrying the so-called "white man's burden" for the rest of the world. This gives us a sense of worth and considerable satisfaction to think

that we are able to help the poverty-stricken, the ignorant, and those without the benefit of the Christian hope. In reality, this not only harms us because it makes us think of ourselves more highly than we ought, fosters self-righteousness on our part in our attitude towards other nations, and causes us to impose ourselves upon others in a kind of neo-colonialism, but it also takes from the very ones we want to assist the most precious possession which they have—their self-respect and sense of worth.[14]

There was little point in seeking to diminish the particular gift and value of the church in the United States. That we could be grateful for the gift of the gospel was borne out in the testimony of those many thousands who had received their legacy of faith in that nation. However, as Clifford emphasized in the course of a dialogue with Alan D. Tyree, reported in the *Saints Herald*:

When we speak of the church in relationship to a country I believe it is important to state that the church is not a political organization. Nor are we a United States church. The church is part of the society where it is located; therefore when we speak of the church in East Germany we speak of a group of persons who are part of a Communist society.[15]

While this may confront the church in some circumstances with some problems of acceptance, or even persecution, the church could still express its peculiar gift in the midst of that society:

I do not perceive the church to be a counter-culture. That assumes that the church has a unique culture. I see the church as a light in every culture. The church brings the judgment of God into the culture and stands to affirm the ultimacy of God and the ultimate worth of persons.[16]

In entering into another culture it might be inevitable that confrontation would occur, bringing basic societal values into conflict. In this situation there was risk not only in the political/cultural disparities, but to the integrity of the gospel:

For that reason we are inclined to say that becoming a world church requires us to plant the seed of the gospel in other lands and take the risk of letting the people there interpret the gospel as it has meaning for them and package it in forms of expression which are indigenous. In some ways we are very uneasy about that kind of freedom, but I remind you that is just the kind of risk God took in planting the Gospel among us.[17]

Autonomy for Every Culture

In the final analysis, it might be that in some cultural environments the basic structures were so firmly rooted, and so incompatible with Christian values, that the flowering of new patterns and allegiances could take place only with great difficulty:

The question was asked in the most recent Asia-Pacific Conference, "Can a Japanese person fully accept the Christian gospel without giving up his Japaneseness?" It may be the answer to that is "no." If it is, however, I am convinced that the initiative for that fundamental cultural change must be from within the Japanese church and cannot be imposed from without. Although our American culture is embedded in centuries of Christian culture we cannot be fully Christian here without giving up much of our Americanness, but that must be done from within. It must not be imposed.[18]

The experience of the church thus far had made it clear that, in the matter of judging the worthiness of other cultures, we would do well to exercise a great measure of humility. One of the factors that stood in the way was our tendency to be largely blind to our own ailments. Merely to indicate some of the values that predominated in the United States and were even widely lauded should be sufficient to suggest caution and suspended judgment. Excessive individualism, aggressiveness, materialism, a youth cult orientation, and mobility were not necessarily compatible with Christian servanthood, even though they might be identified as the "best way."[19]

"I must confess," Clifford concluded, "to having social and spiritual blindness. I am so much a part of this culture that I can only dimly perceive its weaknesses." However, herein was a universal principle to be applied:

> The people of each nation should be intensely loyal to their own culture and nation, but they should also remember that they are a part of a world brotherhood and disciples of the Lord Jesus Christ. All of us must be humble and know that we are not so much in possession of the solution to the world's cultural problems as we are learners in the midst of the world's struggles.... The God who creates in such diversity and finds it good has created and permitted people to create great varieties in cultures, each having characteristics and strengths of profound value based on important truth, and each having weakness, evil, and cultural blindness. As brothers and sisters we can love one another.[20]

The acknowledgment of our own blindness might serve as a dampening effect on our enthusiasm for pursuing the mission of the church far from our own borders, but it should in no way undermine the cause of the gospel. Holding to the universal commitment to the sovereignty of God and the ultimate worth of human beings would enable the church to bring its unique gift wherever it was invited:

> In the Western world the symbols of affluence and success have been associated with meaning. It seems evident that these symbols are not able to sustain meaning. So our role in Western culture is to meet the need persons have for meaning in life. This cannot be solved by substituting some other culture's meaning for our own. There are ultimate meanings in life found in faith in God and the worth of personality. The church offers this in any culture. When these ultimate meanings undergird the life of persons, they are able to keep secondary meanings from becoming idols.[21]

In a powerful parable shared by Clifford and reproduced in the Appendix,[22] Clifford highlighted the need to let initiative for the work reside in each culture as members of the church there responded to the demands and challenges of the gospel.

The Challenge of Pluralism

The foregoing laid the basis for yet another issue, possibly the most stressful of all, and as yet an unfulfilled challenge: the question of cultural diversity—or pluralism in matters of structure, form, and procedures—within the one church. In many respects these questions directed us back to the experience of Peter cited at the beginning of this chapter. As the church entered the 1980s with two decades of experience in other cultures, Clifford issued a major challenge. Would the church make efforts to remain a relatively homogeneous group, socially and economically uniform, upper lower-class and middle-class Caucasian American, with traditionally developed forms of being the church in terms of worship patterns, structures of corporate church life, and other traditions long established in North America? In considering this appealing possibility, Clifford warned that "the world of the future will not accommodate the exclusive church." The outcome of such a stance would inevitably mean extinction or irrelevance. Even in North America this stance might not be the accepted norm of the future if the church was to minister to the several subcultures where its voice and presence had not to that point been particularly effective.[23] The church, in essence, faced a fundamental choice:

> The second alternative is to say that we believe we are the church of Jesus Christ and therefore our fellowship is for all cultures and classes and generations of time. If so, we must develop the kind of pluralism in the church which allows for differences of cultural and economic appreciation and gives latitude in forms of worship and patterns of living. This will be hard to do, but I wonder if it is possible to do anything less and still be the church of Jesus Christ. If at any point our attitude towards others exclude them from our fellowship because of class, cultural, or racial differences, this in itself may be strong evidence that we are not really the church at all. I pray this will never happen.[24]

The question remained to be answered intentionally by the church or unintentionally by default:

> In the long run it may be that we will not pay the price to become a world church. If we do not, our own integrity will require us to minister well to those we have decided to reach and to admit that we are unable to span the range required to be a world church.... For my own part, I believe we are called to be a World Church. I believe we can span the range and will work toward that end.[25]

Notes

1. "The Theology of Mission," an address to high priests and spouses in Independence, Missouri (March 20, 1971), 3–4.
2. Ibid., 2
3. Ibid., 3.
4. "Explorations in Becoming a World Church," in *Saints Herald* (August 1978): 19.
5. Ibid., 20.
6. "The Church in Culture," in *Saints Herald* (June 1977): 12.
7. "Theological Perspectives of World Mission," in *Saints' Herald* (July 1971):10.
8. "The World Church: Our Mission in the 1980's," in *Commission* (September 1979): 44.
9. "Theological Perspectives of World Mission," 13, 60.
10. Ibid., 60. See also "Explorations in Becoming a World Church," 21.
11. "Theological Perspectives of World Mission," 12.
12. "On Being a World Church" (July 1975), 1.
13. "Theological Perspectives of World Mission," 13.
14. Ibid., 60.
15. "The Church in Culture: A Dialogue," in *Saints Herald* (March 1976): 12.
16. Ibid.
17. "Explorations in Becoming a World Church," 20.
18. Ibid.
19. "The Church in Culture," 13–14.
20. Ibid., 43.
21. "The Church in Culture: A Dialogue," 14.

22. "The Church in Culture," 43–44.
23. "On Being a World Church," 2.
24. "Theological Perspectives of World Mission," 62.
25. "Explorations in Becoming a World Church," 43.

■ *CHAPTER 9* ■

The Cause of Zion

In the early years of the church a cluster of images had developed around the concept of "the cause of Zion." The compelling appeal of these images, considered to be thoroughly consistent with prevailing ideas concerning the unique role of North America in the divine purpose had, with the passing of time, virtually assumed the status of dogma and captured a place of primary importance in the understanding and teaching of the Saints. The vision of the new land as a "city set on a hill," or the "New Jerusalem," had inspired early migrants from the Old World, who in many instances endeavored to establish such a "divine commonwealth" in the places where they settled. Nevertheless, the description of the "land of promise" was generally understood to apply to the entire continent, or at least that part of it free from European domination. The image was equally compelling whether evoked in a religious or a political setting.

Very early in the history of the Restoration movement, the city of Independence in, Jackson County, Missouri, was identified as the "center place" for the land of Zion, and succeeding generations of church members nourished this central expectation of "gathering to Zion." In the latter years of the nineteenth century, the words of T. W. Smith's hymn, "Shall We Gather Home to Zion" had a particular appeal. As the commentary on this hymn in *The Hymnal* stated:

> The Saints picked it up and sang it with fervor. Times have changed; the interpretation of Zion has expanded, and these words are not sung with the outlook of former years. It remains, however, the *most* distinctive song of the Saints during those years when the Gathering

seemed delayed but the longing for it was deep in the hearts of those of the early Reorganization.[1]

Nevertheless, when President Frederick M. Smith wrote the words to "Onward to Zion" during the 1922 General Conference, it was clear that although the specifics of the concept may have undergone some change, the fundamental image remained remarkably powerful. The commentary on this hymn, which was also transferred to the historical section of *The Hymnal*, stated: "This song catches up the church's faith in Zion, the dream that will not die."[2]

A Growing Symbol

Although the dream would certainly persist as a prevailing symbol, the particular interpretations clustering around the image would also become more far ranging. It is interesting to note that in a 1968 issue of the *Saints' Herald*, when Clifford offered his evaluation of the concept of Zion, another perspective, substantially different, also appeared over the name of a prominent church leader. In a brief but sharply focused statement, Clifford elaborated on the title of his article, "The Meaning of Zion in Our Time." He began by asserting that early applications of the Zionic vision had not been without problems:

> When the Saints of the early church moved to Independence their concern was not limited to the establishment of an ecclesiastical organization. They were also interested in stores, printing presses, trades, and government. Tremendous problems arose out of the church's control of the economic and social life of its people.... Other unsuccessful attempts based on the Zionic community ideal were recorded at Adam Ondi Ahman, Far West, and eventually Nauvoo.[3]

In responding to the question of why the Saints had been so frequently subjected to opposition and persecution in the early years of the movement, the author ventured the following:

> I would like to suggest that one of the problems originated because the kind of Zionic community the Saints wanted to establish in Independence and Nauvoo could not exist in any sovereign government without conflict. It required such a high degree of autonomy that it could survive only as a separate sovereign state. The ultimate of this can be found in the Nauvoo Charter with its extraordinary governmental powers which even allowed the courts of Nauvoo to countermand the decisions made by other courts.[4]

Clifford remembered his growing years in Wyoming when his parents, along with most of the Saints, eagerly awaited the call from the church authorities that would summon them "home" to Zion. He was aware of the frustration that often existed as the anticipated call to return and help build Zion did not eventuate. Such feelings persisted even though Joseph Smith III had counseled the members to establish themselves in the areas where they lived and become active community builders there:

> In spite of everything that Joseph III said about putting down roots, most of our people in Wyoming could not really feel that they ought to build for permanence there.[5]

Having briefly reviewed some of the inherited traditions, Clifford suggested some fundamental understandings for the future. In the first place, the building of Zion would not be achieved on any other foundation than the life of faith and the shared life of the Saints that supported the purpose of God "to bring to pass the immortality and eternal life of man." There was no great chasm between the mutual sharing of the gifts of the Saints toward this end and the building of Zion:

> The most important element of Zion is what happens to the people who work to create it.... God does not send a hailstorm because he dislikes somebody; rather, he has created the universe in which these problems exist so that men are forced to address themselves to solving them in order to develop qualities which either condemn them or bring to them salvation.... The end value, however, is to be seen in

terms of personality; his supreme purpose is to create in us those qualities of life which are able to endure his presence.[6]

Viewed from this perspective, the Saints were not to feel disillusioned or frustrated if their building of Zion seemed to be delayed. The "cause of Zion" was an ongoing commitment to which the members of any period in time could feel matched. It mattered little whether one served in the first or the last hour of some imagined timeline:

> The scriptures speak of those who saw the city afar off but enjoyed the pleasures of that city through faith. There is a sense in which the church is not only those of us who are living now but those who in centuries past have lived for this cause.... We need to see ourselves as part of that broad movement of God through the centuries. But God has not reserved the joys of Zion for those who come at the end, for the same joys are available to the laborers in each generation. I believe in Zion, but I don't believe in an accomplished Zion which becomes static. If such should ever be, then life would be over; there would be no purpose of living.[7]

The foregoing tended to identify both the kind of ministry called for in the building of Zion and the places where that ministry should be extended:

> Now, having said these things about Zion, I hasten to add that we should address ourselves at this particular period of history to doing those things which God has created us to do...these include creating godly communities with good school systems, wise political organizations, and fair employment opportunities. It addresses the problems of the ghettos; members of the church are called to become a part of the communities in which they live so that rather than being isolated from the world they see themselves as entering the world as disciples of Jesus Christ. They touch the lives of others in the community like leaven. The church is called not to save itself but to...be in the world in such a way that its influence will bring the world to God.[8]

Clifford expanded this broader view of Zion in a seminar of church leaders in December 1974. The vision of a transformed and sacralized society was expressed in many forms, revealing the most profound hope of humankind.

Such a vision was not foreign to the Christian hope, nor to the members of the Restoration movement. Referring to the many ways human beings had nourished this hope, Clifford stated that

> the fact of bringing the vision of paradise down from heaven to be achieved here on earth is not out of keeping with our Christian heritage. Jesus taught his disciples to pray, "Thy kingdom come, thy will be done on earth as it is in heaven," and the many references of Jesus preaching the gospel of the kingdom as well as his prophecy that "this gospel of the kingdom shall be preached in all the world for a witness unto all nations, and then shall come the end" bears ample witness that Christ gave a major emphasis to the importance of an earthly kingdom of God.[9]

In contrast to the central teaching of the New Testament, the Old Testament view of the kingdom involved the chosen nation and was centered in Jerusalem. Yet even in the New Testament, and among some of the primary witnesses to the gospel, prejudices of national exclusiveness or chosenness exerted their pull against the commitment to a mission devoted to world renewal.

A Land of Promise?

Against the background of the struggle in sixteenth-, seventeenth-, and eighteenth-century Europe to emerge from the bondage of the feudal system, the newly "discovered" land of America met a cherished hope in the minds of many people:

> Common people saw in America a dream within reach where they could own their own land and be as the lords. They came as indentured servants, some bought their passage, some were even sent from prison to populate the New Colonies.... In all of this, however, it is important for us to see that the upheaval in Europe had not only given hope to the common person, and caused him to challenge tradition, but this also led to war, misery, and discontent with conditions as they were. This combination of discontent with the accompanying dream of a better life where the problems and injus-

tices of their world could be eradicated, stimulated hopes for the perfect society.[10]

The vision of a perfected society committed to building the kingdom of God in the promised land brought Puritans, Quakers, Catholics, and others who saw themselves fulfilling the biblical image of the "city set on a hill" and committed to restoring the ancient order of things.[11]

It is not possible to understand the development of Zionic concepts and ideals in the early Restoration church without taking into account the historical influences of preceding centuries in the "Old World"—the term "old" signifying not so much antiquity as moral and political degeneration. Such an understanding is important and indeed indispensable

> [to] help us get a sense of the social, political, economic and religious sense out of which Joseph Smith and the early Saints emerged and the forces that guided their thinking about Zion. Without in any sense denying the influence of the divine in bringing the new church into existence or, for that matter, shaping the larger world developments that we have brought into focus, it is my belief that the concepts and objectives of Latter Day Saints were powerfully influenced by European and American history. In a very real sense our movement was conceived and nurtured in the climate of the Utopian dream of a perfect society. We were the inheritors of the belief that America was somehow preserved by God for the purpose of establishing the kingdom. We were assured that the laws and constitution of the United States were divinely achieved and preserved.[12]

Although Independence and Jackson County remained central in the mind of Joseph Smith, the vision was enlarged before his death to embrace all of the United States of America, a vision that was paralleled on the political level by the decision to enter his candidacy for president of the United States.

Agenda for a Growing Church

The balance of this presentation was given to identify eight questions that Clifford considered crucial for the church to consider. The questions are reproduced verbatim here:

> Firstly, in the light of history and the Scriptures what do we conceive to be our ultimate Zionic objectives?
>
> Secondly, how do we today view the Old Testament images and models used in the early church to relate us to an isolated, self-autonomous, exclusive Zion?
>
> Thirdly, what place do we give today to the Christian concept of Zion as the leaven, light, or salt that enters the world to transform society?
>
> Fourthly, how does the church today view the significance of the primitive church and the Scripture as the guide for Zionic development and in what ways are we free to move out into the dynamic world around us unfettered by the past?
>
> Fifthly, to what extent have we, like the early Americans, found ourselves ambivalent about our spiritual and theological objectives and therefore increasingly oriented toward achieving economic prosperity, personal security and the so-called good-life?
>
> Sixthly, how does the church, which is so rooted in the American heritage, relate itself Zionically to the world and more especially to that part of the world which does not share the heritage of...the Great American Experiment which we know as the United States?
>
> Seventhly, if Zion is to deal with the frontiers of society and see itself as a concretion of God's action where growth and change is taking place, how do we identify the new frontiers and call the church to address these as God's people in mission?
>
> Eighthly, whatever our Zionic objectives may be how can we realistically break the task down into achievable steps so that our people can be released from frustration and guilt for not accomplishing the impossible and find satisfaction and joy in their discipleship?[13]

The foregoing catalog of issues made up a formidable agenda for leaders and members of the church. It was not possible for the church to undertake a serious review of its mission independently of the questions relating to Zion:

> It is my considered judgment that the first obvious area to consider in the light of our times is the concept of Zion. Firstly because we are carrying the freight of an idea packaged on the other side of the divide.[14] For most of our people the notion of a geographic commu-

nity on a sacred piece of geography dominated by Latter Day Saint influences and characterized by a perfection of social governmental and economic relationships is still the goal. In the early days of the Latter Day Saint movement we saw ourselves implementing the zionic idea in the time honored fashion, i.e., being called to a new land, divinely designated as a land of promise, to become a "chosen people," a "Latter Day Israel," a "City set on a hill" as a light to the world. As a middle principle it was a viable pattern to follow. However, the danger is that the middle principle for a past era will be considered an ultimate and hence pressed down upon another generation or culture where it does not fit....[15]

Notwithstanding the cautions that had been raised, the fundamental call to establish the cause of Zion was still both powerful in its appeal and appropriate to the mission to which the Saints were called. Like all valid symbols, it required reinterpretation as the historical and cultural circumstances changed, yet still had the power to draw the people of God to commitment:

In short, I am proposing that for us Zion must become a lived-out principle that God is involved in, and concerned with, all of life. Therefore, he is quite as much concerned about the secular relations of people as he is about their worship. He is the God of the street, the market place, the legislative hall, the factory and the hospital. Because this is so the prophetic church must also be involved with, and speak to, the totality of life.[16]

Power in Gathering

One of the most persistent and valuable concepts of the Zionic theme is that of the *Gathering*. Perhaps members had perceived the need to reinterpret this theme and had been prepared to live it in the reality of their present experience, rather than being bound to a traditional understanding. In his book *Faith for New Frontiers* Clifford lifted up the central importance of this principle as vital to "keeping the faith," strengthening the resolve of the Saints, and sharpening the focus of the Zionic witness:

> The principle of the Gathering is essential to the maintenance of the faith. This means not only that the development of Zionic communities at the Center Place is important, but that the branch in any part of the world is also an expression of the Gathering. As people congregate, associating together in wholesome activities, they impart to each other and their children the contagious faith they share. When sufficient numbers of our people live in close proximity to share in some aspects of social, recreational, and economic life as well as religious life, they are reaping some of the benefits implicit in the Gathering itself.[17]

As the church grew and established concentrations of members in many locations the value of gathering became increasingly clear. At the Conference of High Priests and Seventies in 1971, Clifford elaborated on the abiding relevance of this principle:

> It was only a few years ago that most church members thought of Zion as being that divinely directed development which was to take place in Jackson County, Missouri, and the surrounding areas, led by the First Presidency and the Presiding Bishopric. Many watched from Conference to Conference for some word from the Lord which would indicate that the implementation of Zion was at hand, or for some action by the general church officers which would open the way to begin actively participating in the building of Zion. Today it is recognized that the principles of Zionic building are worldwide in scope. Every stake is basically organized and empowered to be about the building of Zion within the geographic area of its boundary. The stake has prophetic resources in its presidency, the economic and social management resident within its bishopric, the wisdom of its high council, the strength of concentrated membership, and the power to mobilize resources for achieving the Zionic goals within its limits. This is decentralization of the very most important kind; it liberates us to be about the business of building Zion.[18]

The principle of the Gathering, interpreted in its broader and more universal sense, was at the heart of the church's outreach:

> Today there is a growing recognition that the cause of Zion is a worldwide cause. Its principles are applicable in all the world. The call of

the church is to go into the world to make disciples in every land and that these disciples should involve themselves as Saints in the communities and nations where they live. As they gather together in communities, as Saints have always done, the ministries possible in a gathered condition and the resources available through strong centers can make these communities effectual in significant ways in the world.[19]

Facing the Future

Despite significant advances in understandings of the Zionic mission, challenges that were in some sense new invited sustained attention. In the first place, it had become common to suggest that Zionic communities should serve as *demonstration* centers. However, as the church moved into other cultures, as described in the previous chapter, the question, "Demonstrations of what?" arose. Should the norm be the middle-class, single-family, suburban, appliance-laden communities so common in the Unites States and other developed Western nations? Or should those cultures in which the village-style extended family prevailed provide the ideal living pattern for a Zionic-minded people? In a paper published in *Commission* magazine (September 1980), Clifford highlighted the issue:

> The demonstration community certainly has a validity but it also has great limitations. The limitations are evident because:
> a. There are few places for developing such communities. The world is far too thoroughly explored and developed to expect any place to be long isolated from the impact of world-wide forces. The experience of those cults which have gone to some remote place for developing a special demonstration is not encouraging.
> b. As a church we do not have the resources either in capital or skill to develop communities which will speak significantly to the world. We need the contributions of the larger world as much as they need ours.[20]

A third factor, and in some ways the most formidable for a church only recently entering the struggle to embrace a multicultured membership, was emerging as a major question to be pressed against the Zionic idea:

> In the diverse cultures and environments of the world a demonstration community in one culture or place is very limited in its value to another. For example, a demonstration community in a rural stake such as Lamoni has only limited value to the solution of problems confronted by the stakes in metropolitan Los Angeles or even Kansas City. It will have even less to say to the people of India. Nevertheless, the principles of Zion or of the revelation God has given us in Jesus Christ may speak to every land and culture when allowed to be interpreted by them and applied in their setting.[21]

Perhaps one issue was and continues to be almost too painful to consider—better and safer merely to follow the established pattern and not be too concerned about the future. In the course of raising contemporary questions for the church in 1974, Clifford described an underlying choice concerning the new frontiers to be forged by people following the Zionic vision:

> This may be raising the question as to whether or not an institution is able to continue on the growing edge of human development. Is it possible that all institutions, like people, in time develop a vested interest in preserving the status quo both in form and in concept, and as a result revolutionary renewals spawning new institutions inevitably take place from time to time to break out of past molds and allow for new growth?[22]

In his last major statement (1980) on the subject of the church's mission, Clifford outlined five major challenges before the church. Each of these pointed to a different aspect of the mission, yet all had implications for the expression of the cause of Zion. While these issues were truly significant, even daunting, Clifford's strong faith was again evident:

> As we look at the past we are impressed with the fact that divine direction and divine forces unforeseen emerge to accomplish the will of God. It is my own faith that the church will not be left alone in the

struggle but that God will continue to be involved in the church and the world to bring to pass his purposes. One of the exciting factors in that struggle is that we never know what amazing and unexpected thing God will do next.[23]

Notes

1. *The Hymnal* (1956), included as No. 579 in the "Historical Hymns" of the church.
2. Ibid., No. 577.
3. "The Meaning of Zion in Our Time," in *Saints' Herald* (May 15, 1968): 10.
4. Ibid.
5. Ibid.
6. Ibid., 11.
7. Ibid.
8. Ibid.
9. "The Scriptural and Historical View of Zion," seminar paper (December 1974), 3.
10. Ibid., 4–5.
11. Ibid., 6.
12. Ibid., 7.
13. Ibid., 9–11.
14. "The "divide" referred to here was the major step taken by the church in opening missions in non-Christian cultures in the 1960s.
15. "Meaning of the Church as Leaven," presented at a meeting of the Joint Council (March 1977), 8–9.
16. Ibid., 9.
17. *Faith for New Frontiers*, 66–67.
18. "Theological Perspectives of World Mission," in *Saints' Herald* (July 1971): 12.
19. "The Doctrine of the Church" (n.d.), 12.
20. "The World Church: Our Mission in the 1980's," in *Commission* (September 1979): 44.
21. Ibid., 44–45.
22. "The Scriptural and Historical View of Zion," 11.
23. "The World Church: Our Mission in the 1980's," 46.

CHAPTER 10

With Eyes on the Horizon

Clifford Cole addressed each World Conference between 1966 and 1980 as president of the Council of Twelve. With one exception these presentations were published in the *Saints Herald*. Because to a high degree they represent the support of members of the council, they reflect both the concerted thinking of that group, and the forward-looking initiative of their president. A review of these eight sermons strongly conveys the impression that they embodied a striking commentary on the progress of the church during those critical years. Indeed, they might be termed, from one point of view, a "state of the church's mission" series. For that reason, and because they embody the spirit of prophecy in the best sense, they are grouped here under the title that heads this chapter.

Our Opportunity for Greatness (1966)

The basic theme for this message was that "Zionic conditions are no further away nor any closer than the spiritual condition of [God's] people justifies." Clifford was able to report a growth in understanding and mutual support among the members of the Council of Twelve and between the general officers of the church. This encouraging condition extended into the field, including those missions opened up since the initial venture in 1960. Citing his visits to a number of these new nations, Clifford stated:

> In these places I have repeatedly been impressed with the knowledge that God anticipates us, sometimes prods us, continually out-

runs us, and often surprises us by the exercise of his might in ways which are deep and powerful to change men's lives and to plant his work in all parts of the world. The miraculous way in which he has touched the hearts of people in other lands, the courage and wisdom which he has given them, and the shared experiences of the Spirit which unite us in understanding and bridges the enormous gaps of language and cultural differences, have been no less amazing than the experiences of the early church.[1]

The church was blessed, Clifford was assured, by a flexibility that enabled it to adjust to the changing circumstances, newly perceived truths, and challenges of the times. Past failures did not discount the power of the church, but rather the impotence of those who were slow to use what God had put into their hands:

> To those who may have felt that we are hopelessly outmoded and unable to speak to the relevant issues of our time, let me say that the body of the church has within it the power to speak prophetically to the world of our day, but these people must not predetermine what God should say or try to use the church to accomplish their particular crusades. And to those who may look back with a kind of nostalgia to the past I would say that the church is a living organism and living organisms cannot be frozen. Any attempt to do so will kill the very life which is to be preserved.[2]

It was a momentous day in the life of the church; the opportunity to serve had never been greater. Drawing attention to the previous six years and the extension of the mission into non-Christian cultures, Clifford said:

> There was a day when our missionary work centered around those beliefs of the church which set us apart from other Christian denominations. This must no longer determine our missionary message. People are not saved by the ways in which they are different from someone else but by their faith in Jesus Christ, their commitment to him, and their acceptance of the full Christian gospel.[3]

At this time we were on the threshold of achieving something that had spoken more of our ambition than our performance: the adventure of becoming, in reality, a *world* church. Accordingly, the church was challenged to put into practice some fundamental principles with a new sense of urgency. These revolved around the readiness of the established church to extend to every culture the responsibility for the conduct and, as far as possible, the financing of the church in its indigenous setting. This should be done in such a way as to avoid some attitudes and practices that, under the guise of well-meaning benevolence, had tended to rob people of their dignity and sense of worth.[4]

Recalling the experience of members in newly established missions, often under persecution, Clifford offered his testimony:

> I still hear the voices of men and women in far-off places singing their songs of praise to almighty God and thanking him for the joy they have found in the restored gospel. Those voices speak a prophecy of a new day in which the little stone cut out of the mountain without hands shall surely fill the whole earth.[5]

The Church of Jesus Christ Confronting Its Mission (1968)

As the general officers were considering the significance of three seminars just completed, as Basic Beliefs Committee was finalizing its work for publication and the "new curriculum controversy" was warming up, Clifford again held up the urgency of the church's mission. Reminding the Conference of the presentation of a Statement of Objectives, two years previously, he reported that "the Joint Council has aggressively tried to pursue the course these objectives indicated, and it is with sober yet thankful hearts that we of the Council of Twelve now bear our witness to you that God has blessed us abundantly in our efforts."[6]

The times, Clifford believed, were critical. Referring to Joseph Smith's record of some of the early experiences, he wrote:

> The difficulties in recovering the founding experiences of the early church with any degree of exactness should caution us to be modest in our claims and humble about our knowledge of the details of those experiences. Nevertheless, one cannot escape the feeling that the men and women who were involved in these experiences responded under an awesome sense of divine mission. Although they were unpretentious people, they stood tall because they knew God had singled them out for a mighty work, and they were therefore marked by the call of destiny.... We can never repay the men and women of the early church, who, through their discipleship, created and transmitted to us the heritage we have.... [L]et no one ever forget that those men and women were grasped by a power which so profoundly changed and empowered their lives that they built cities, conquered undeveloped areas, endured privation and persecution, and exerted a major influence on a developing nation....[7]

The debt to our predecessors was incalculable, and should inspire an equally committed response in our own situation. To be grateful for the past, however, was not to try to reproduce it:

> There is, of course, a kind of unhealthy preoccupation with the church and the sacred events of the past which can direct our attention away from the issues of our time. Our fathers nobly responded to the call of God in their generation, but we cannot suppose that devotion to their successes will serve the present needs of mankind. If our only hope is in recapturing the past, then we are already dead and the basic principles by which a living, vibrating church was born have already been lost.[8]

Although the modern world held formidable dangers, it was still God's world. "The church must not," Clifford warned, "be dragged whimpering and protesting into the world God is creating." Some possibilities were indeed daunting: a profound change in fundamental economic processes, rapid population growth, the dehumanizing effect of a mechanized society, and the problems of helping people find a sense of worth and purpose for being:

> We might go on with descriptions of other developments which are appearing on the horizon to indicate the kind of new world which is

dawning. Some of these involve a technology which will increase and heighten intelligence or stultify the mind. Some have to do with prolonging life and such ambivalent issues as that of determining when a person ought to be allowed to die in peace, rather than maintaining life by artificial means. The new world emerging before us is awesome and the potentiality for both good and ill staggers the mind.[9]

The church was called to be prophetic in the midst of unsettling changes and unpredictable outcomes. In a time when people were separating the sacred from the secular, prizing the secular and dismissing God to the edges of life—if at all—the cause of Zion became increasingly important, to lift up the understanding that "spirit and element" were inseparably joined to minister to the whole of life.

With the same courage and sense of calling exhibited by the Saints of another time, the members of the present time were empowered to join skill and devotion for the sake of the gospel:

The church is called to an exacting, but glorious mission in this time. When we look at our heritage we are profoundly grateful for it. When we stand on the watchtowers of our times we are awed by the amazing developments which are sweeping us into an unplumbed and uncharted future, but we are eternally thankful that God has matched us with this day. Like Young Joseph in Palmyra, we are sometimes confused, but our heritage reminds us that he was impressed with the amazing promise he read in James 1:5. From the exercise of that promise there emerged a marvelous work. But the promise was not for that day only. This day as well as that demands of us an undaunted faith in God.[10]

The Great Witnesses (1970)

At a time when internal stresses that had existed for almost two decades were reaching a new intensity, Clifford addressed the Conference to affirm the church's fundamental convictions. Acknowledging the internal struggles, he began by stating the following:

All of us at times feel threatened when our traditions are tested.... We should never fear evaluation and testing, but we must not become preoccupied with it either. We want to speak as honestly as we can about the convictions that have sustained the church in times past and will support us in the future.[11]

In such an uncertain time it was important to reaffirm belief in God, with the assurance that God "is able to keep his own," that "no evil in the long run can defeat his purposes.[12] Further, and standing alongside this affirmation, was the church's testimony of a living Christ:

> Belief in the living Christ has always characterized our movement and is a part of our heritage.... Perhaps it has never been more true than now. As the men of the Council of Twelve have returned from fields in Argentina, India, Haiti, French Polynesia, and other places throughout the world they have borne testimony of the power of Christ directing ministry to those who have searched for him.[13]

It was the enduring power of these foundations that permitted us to affirm our faith in the church. Despite charges of irrelevance or opposition driven by the forces of self-interest and outright evil, the church stood to do what it was called to do under God:

> There are many unresolved problems in the world. There are unresolved problems in the church and in our homes and personal lives also. In the midst of this frustration and inequity we all have a disposition to lay blame on something, and the church is the object of an inordinate share of this criticism. We have no disposition to be defensive about this. Inasmuch as the church can give ministry to resolve these problems and heal the sickness in the world, it should; and where it is failing to do so, it needs to repent.[14]

"We need the church," said Clifford, "because it is the body which has preserved and transmitted the memory of God's movement in history."[15] To affirm this was to affirm the importance and value of the scriptures. He acknowledged that there had been some questions raised about long-held assumptions concerning the Book of Mormon. Members should not shrink from opening our claims to honest investigation, and they should not be satisfied with anything less. At the same time, we stand firmly on our testimony:

> Just as we were able to say that one powerful evidence of the validity of the church was the quality of the influence it shed on the lives of its members, so we must say the testimony of the life lived by the teaching and spirit of the Book of Mormon bears witness to its truth and its value. I have never known anyone who tried to live by the principles taught in the Book of Mormon who wasn't a better, happier, and a more godly person as a result. The influence of the book upon those who follow its teachings is one of the most powerful evidences of its validity.[16]

As was his custom in addressing the Conference, or any other group for that matter, Clifford concluded with his strong testimony:

> We have now grown to be a strong church. We are recognized in the world so that we no longer are confronted with the threat of extinction. We do not need any longer to justify that fact. No outside enemy can defeat us. Only we can do that. If either inner conflict or unfaithfulness to our mission seeps into our structure we are in danger, but if we remain true to our calling no power can stop us. God is at our right hand. He is our savior and the assurance of victory.[17]

Called into This Time (1972)

As on previous occasions, this address called the Saints to enter fully and confidently into the church's mission in the current time—challenging and uncertain admittedly, but no less dynamic and exciting than the time in which the church was founded. Referring to the various discordant voices raised tending to weaken the resolve of the Saints, Clifford said:

> Our faith in God, however, will not allow us to believe that we are abandoned or that he has led us to this place to destroy us. Neither do we believe he has led the church to this place in history and given us such a multitude of evidences of his love and direction to allow it to be destroyed by enemies from without or within.[18]

Clifford described how the confidence in science, knowledge, and technology had lured societies into an unbounded optimism regarding the future, a confidence that had been utterly shattered by the experiences of depression, war, and persisting injustice. In light of the despair that was so prevalent, the church could not be content with a message that failed to speak realistically and directly to human need:

> It is not likely that the church in this generation can command the attention of a weary and desperate world with a view based on the beliefs of the nineteenth and early twentieth centuries with their strong emphasis on a doctrine of other-worldliness. It is not enough for the church today to hold out the promise of an escape from this world with its troubles and extend only the hope that the in-justices of the present will be righted in a life beyond the grave.[19]

The call to declare a God who was involved in this present world was another way of lifting up the cause of Zion. However, the church's message of Zion was not a restatement of the Old Testament image of a chosen nation with its exclusivism. Nor was it so dominantly eschatological, looking to some future time for realization that anything less yielded frustration:

> It is possible for us to become so enamored with our anticipation of the fulfillment of God's purposes at the "end of the age" and so anxious to achieve the promises of that ultimate vision that we ignore the intermediate tasks which help us come to grips with the Zionic imperatives for our generation.... If we can now keep the vision of the consummation toward which God moves out there before us, and at the same time identify the in-between steps which should be taken in this generation, we may be released from the frustrations that have characterized our Zionic enterprise and find the satisfaction of some successes.[20]

A second major challenge facing the Saints was that of becoming a world church. Citing the tendency of denominations to become homogenous in membership and cultural pattern, Clifford reminded the Conference participants that they were even then facing questions regarding the ability of the church to tolerate ways of life and social patterns different from the dominant Western cultures. Strains could even arise from differences that had little to do with basic Christian commitments

> However, if we are unable to tolerate and accept into full fellowship those who may worship differently and who live by patterns of life different from ours, then it is very clear that we cannot hope to become a worldwide church, nor can God depend on us to represent him fully among all cultures.[21]

This stance would not only affect those in faraway places, but those within the "domestic" field, who tended to be excluded, no matter how subtly, and were not embraced in the fellowship:

> If we choose to ignore the problem, then we have answered it—and our answer is a clear decision to become not a world church but an institution of homogeneous people of similar class and cultural preference, limited to those already of our orientation or those we can change to become like us.[22]

Clifford invited the Conference to take full appreciation of its heritage of continuing revelation. This could protect the institution from the temptation to "solidify itself into one particular frame of history, holding fast to that structure and theology long after their usefulness is past." Our longstanding trust in a revealing God was at once a blessing and a challenge:

> We are not called to restore the past but to restore the vital relationship with God.... In a practical way this means the church is always caught in the tension between the experience of the past and the uncharted future.... We are required by our calling to live with God in such a way that we are free to examine ourselves, the church, and our society without the fear that such an examination will destroy us. This means we must have the courage to leave that which ought to be left and to see our own vested interests for what they are.[23]

We could truly believe that we were called into this time rather than to some other, past or future. Should this be indeed true,

> The great question is not, "How soon shall God bring the fulfillment of the age and end the work which he has laid upon us?" but "Will we be found faithful in doing his work in that period of history which has been matched against us?" We have been called into this time. Let it be said that we are faithful to that call.[24]

The Cause of Zion Today and Tomorrow (1974)

This sermon, summarizing Clifford's thought concerning Zion, received the Elbert A. Smith Memorial Award for 1974. Introducing the statement, Clifford said:

> We believe that we should take stock of our course from time to time to see clearly how we arrived at our present position and where our direction will carry us. As we have done this, we want now to share with you some of the trends that concern us and some of the opportunities which we must not avoid.[25]

Briefly Clifford traced several historical developments that shaped the environment in which the Restoration movement came into being. These included the concern with otherworldliness, the importance of authority, the validity of exclusiveness (the "one true church" motif), the appeal of the promise of the kingdom of God, and more generally in the early history of the United States, the belief in "manifest destiny." In the early nineteenth century the broader "restoration" movement had impelled a number of religious groups to attempt the recovery of the primitive church in fullness and purity, as characterized by Thomas Campbell's 1809 "Declaration and Address." While none of these factors, nor all of them together, could in any sense be said to have "caused" our movement, they could not be dismissed as if they had no bearing on the origin and shaping of the church. However they might be evaluated, the focus of attention had altered.

> Where once we were preoccupied with recapturing the past, now we are increasingly absorbed in restoring and revitalizing our relationship to God and his purpose.... It is important for us to continue the stance bequeathed to us by the founders of the movement—not that we back into the future with eyes intent on the issues of a past generation, not that we commit our resources to defending our convictions about our past history, but that we speak to our day as the body of Christ.[26]

The movement of history had also brought a confident—though from hindsight a naïve—trust in science and progress. More recent events had sobered, confused, and distressed those who were inadequately prepared for the "new" world of the twentieth century. This was a time of opportunity for the church:

> We are a part of a complex and an amazing panorama of God's action. This is Christ's church, but it is so in the midst of Christ's world; and as we look back now on our past, we wonder if such gripping statements as, "Now, behold, a marvelous work is about to come forth among the children of men" really didn't have far wider connotations than either the founders of the church or we ourselves have realized.[27]

A new world was being born, Clifford asserted, requiring a new kind of people to live in it. Without attempting to predict the shape of the future, an undertaking that had thus far proved notoriously unsuccessful, he shared some convictions concerning what the church had to offer in this new world. These he expressed in four challenges:[28]

1. a deep commitment to the faith and a total immersion in the life it demanded;

2. a turning outward to confront crucial conditions as a leavening presence;

3. a truly evangelizing church, winning people to the values and commitments of Christ; and

4. a movement toward becoming an enabling church, with greater initiative for national and local jurisdictions.

Speaking as president of the Council of Twelve, Clifford issued a call to mission, not to be accepted with trepidation but with full confidence:

> We believe that this is a crucial time for [the church] to grasp the larger challenges God is laying at its door. We believe we have a unique history and resources for the call that is beckoning us today. To be called by God to such an hour as this is a most exciting and demanding opportunity.[29]

On Being the Body of Christ (1976)

Referring to the apostle Paul's analogy describing the church as a body, Clifford proceeded to draw some implications for the contemporary church. First of all was the need for unity in the body. The apostle Paul observed that the spirit that should have united the newly formed congregations of the young church appeared to have become the cause for division. Accordingly he insisted that although members may differ in their gifts, the Spirit maintained the church as a single organism. There was a clear lesson for the contemporary church:

> There is need for testing, exploring, and healthy debate in the Body of Christ, but there is no place where one part of the body can reject another without damage to the whole. The concept of the body makes it clear that life depends on mutual support.[30]

Extending this analogy Clifford applied it to the need to establish a healthy relationship with the rest of humanity and with those other denominations composing the Christian witness. "Particularly during the past decade," he stated, "God has been moving in the church to call us to this larger responsibility." This was not being achieved without concern on the part of some members:

> Probably the greatest fear generated among us when we talk of the need to enter into common endeavors with peoples and organizations in the world around us is that we shall lose our Latter Day

> Saint distinctives, faith, and practice.... I am concerned too, but I cannot believe we are so weak or vague about our own commitment that we are unable to maintain our essential faith while we enter into the world and become the leaven to transform it under the power of God who is commissioning us to go.[31]

Strengthened by the disciplines of devotion and prayer and "aware of the sweep and expanse of the solemnity of eternity," members could enter a precarious and threatening world with an underlying calm and freedom from fear that carried with it an assurance of ultimate victory. This enabled the Saints to live with the ability to adapt to the times and the call of God to our times:

> It is precisely because the church functions as a living body that we have great confidence that it will not only survive the tremendous changes but be able to minister to a world in the agony of such travail. Those forms of life that were less adequately endowed with powers of evaluation and adaptation to a changing environment are or will be numbered among the extinct species. They are the dinosaurs, mammoths, and the saber-toothed tigers whose remains testify of a time now past.[32]

Acknowledging that the "adjustments and uncertainties of the last two decades" had muted evangelistic outreach, Clifford reminded the Conference that a healthy body needed to be growing. This indicated the need for an energetic and informed missionary witness. In such a world as was emerging the church might be tempted to settle for less:

> In the midst of these great world-shaking and culture-shocking movements we could well let an unhealthy religion become our way of copping out. Feeling inadequate and overwhelmed we could thrust the shaping of our world into the hands of God and take refuge in an anti-rational and anti-intellectual haven, waiting for God to intervene and overturn all human efforts and set up his own kingdom.[33]

Even though we may at times doubt our own ability to match such awesome responsibilities, this was no time for a failure of nerve:

We are convinced that God will not shield us from the future, and the greatest tragedy we could choose would be to turn aside from the door of the emerging world, in an attempt to conserve the past, under the mistaken notion that this offers security. It would be like a pilot in flight losing nerve and shutting down his motors in an attempt to find a stationary position of stability in midair. This is a dynamic world, and we move into the future by faith—not discounting the risk but knowing there is no other viable course.[34]

On Choosing Life (1978)

Given the fact that the church had not escaped the "conflict or traumatic uncertainties" which had beset the world in general, the temptation facing members might be the "disposition to cry out now for a new Moses to lead us through the uncertain time into the 'promised kingdom.'"[35]

In the larger sense...prophetic leaders emerge when they are lifted up on the shoulders of a prophetic people.... In a very practical way we call the church at this historic Conference to thank God for the leadership he has given us both in the past and the present and to insightfully support that leadership in the future.... [B]eyond this, however, the whole church is called to struggle together to break new ground for the kingdom of God yet in the future.[36]

Rather than attempting "to plow new furrows where we don't want them," it was timely to determine where we were and where we wanted to go. Given the circumstances in which the church was brought forth, there was a lingering tendency to act from a defensive posture to "prove" that the claims of the church were true. In demonstrating the folly of such a stance in the church's evangelistic outreach, Clifford offered an illustration:

A recent comic strip showed Dagwood at the door meeting a salesman who was selling icebox pans. The salesman explained how the pan was placed under the icebox to catch the drip from the melting ice. Dagwood responded by saying, "Haven't you heard of the refrigerator?" "No," said the salesman, "I've been busy inventing this icebox pan!"[37]

This did not mean that there was no place either for the traditional foundations of the message or for some of the methods used earlier to attract interest. Nevertheless:

> It does mean that trying to prove the validity of the church by past methods is generally unproductive if not counterproductive.... If we assume then that God is at work saving the people of the world through reconciliation to him and to each other, and has called us to be an instrument in his hands to bring that salvation about, then our mission must also center in that cause. The question today is not so much one of proving the validity or truth of the church as it is to *be* the true and valid church. The latter is ever so much harder.[38]

Moving from a consideration of the essentials to more fully being the Church of Jesus Christ, Clifford lifted up several "musts."[39] The church must move away from the view that the world is our adversary and be "supportive of good wherever it emerges." The gospel to be proclaimed must offer wholeness, hope, and victory in Christ, avoiding any emphasis on the fear of doom or calamity. The nature and role of community, central to our heritage, must receive renewed attention. We must be a "person-building" church. Of this need, he said:

> My purpose in raising this issue is to affirm our growing belief that the salvation of our world now rests significantly more in the realm of the spirit rather than in the achievement of the "flesh."[40]

We must be a praying church, Clifford added, both for our own sake and the sake of those for whom we pray. Finally, we must really want to grow and expand, with programs that embrace new members, avoid the "in-house" language that tends to exclude people different from us, and free them to express their giftedness in our midst.

Poised between Eras (1980)

In his final Conference address, at the sesquicentennial

gathering, Clifford reiterated his conviction that we are living during an "in-between" time:

> There are ways in which the limitations of our past and the uncertainties of the future have fallen more sharply into focus since the Conference of 1978, but we are still symbolically standing on tiptoe anticipating the new and better day.[41]

In past times, he stated, primary value was accorded economic growth, competition, progress, and achievement. These values had been so implicit as to require little examination. However, this may be a time for holding these values up to scrutiny:

> In more recent years new values of human worth and personal freedom have come into our world. The inequity of uneven distribution of wealth, the social problems of poverty, ignorance, disease, and starvation have become foremost in our concern.[42]

Even the promise of such liberal political and economic concepts written in the United States in political programs has fallen short of the hoped-for outcomes, and in many ways "our permissiveness had turned sour." Under the broad theme of stewardship, embracing the cultivation, management, and responsibility for the earth, the church in its heritage and understanding could make a significant contribution. A fundamental attitude, established in our scripture, emphasizes humility and love as basic disciplines if the members are to function effectively as a leavening presence in the world. Further, Latter Day Saint scripture emphasizes the importance of competence in performance:

> Intelligence, we are told, is "the glory of God." Accepting responsibility for the use of intelligence is difficult. I have always believed in spiritual or numinous experience.... My concern, however, is that in many cases good Saints, as well as others, use a pseudo spiritualism as an escape from the hard realities of work and personal responsibility.[43]

Pursuing the theme of stewardship, Clifford identified a new challenge, which both Christian and non-Christians had been slow to address: an appropriate response to the command to "be fruitful and multiply."

> In the past the question has often revolved around "moral or immoral" issues. We had "highly emotional" words to describe these concerns—adultery, polygamy, chastity, monogamy, and the like. However, the unrestrained size of a family when children were conceived by wedded husband and wife in a monogamous family was approved. In fact, in some religious organizations it was encouraged. If the world of the future is to do away with war, disease, and famine, the control of family size is imperative.[44]

Another primary concern arose, growing out of a perceived scriptural base, but taking on a new perspective in the view of the developing situation, and in the light of the human tendency to interpret "dominion" as "exploitation":

> The matter of dominion over the resources of the world and of subduing it is also in the process of reevaluation. In our Western mode of dealing with the world's resources we have emphasized the concept of subduing. We have talked of taming the rivers, conquering the wild frontier, and harnessing power. It's as if the chaos of the natural world has been waiting to be brought into order by human strength and ingenuity.... Looking back on the period, we see that some of those interpretations were misguided, and that Christian theology has been used to justify the unrestrained exploitation of the natural world in ways that now confront us with terrible consequences.[45]

Recent developments had brought this disposition to exploitation seriously under question and added a new dimension to the principle of stewardship, as indicated in Doctrine and Covenants 150:7:

> Today we express concern that a more just distribution be made of the world's resources and that the church should be leading and leavening the decision-making bodies in helping achieve this end.... In the years ahead we, as a church, should be in the forefront of such

movements. We should do this not only because we are God's people, but because—in a very rational way—our salvation as well as that of the world depends on it.[46]

Notes

1. "Our Opportunities for Greatness," in *Saints' Herald* (June 15, 1966): 6.
2. Ibid.
3. Ibid., 8.
4. Ibid., 8, 20.
5. Ibid., 20.
6. "The Church of Jesus Christ Confronting Its Mission," unpublished sermon transcript, 1.
7. Ibid., 2–3.
8. Ibid., 3–4.
9. Ibid., 8.
10. Ibid., 14–15.
11. "The Great Witnesses," in *Saints' Herald* (September 1970): 14.
12. Ibid.
13. Ibid., 15.
14. Ibid.
15. Ibid., 16.
16. Ibid.
17. Ibid., 18.
18. "Called Into This time," in *Saints Herald* (June 1972): 10.
19. Ibid., 11.
20. Ibid., 46.
21. Ibid., 47.
22. Ibid.
23. Ibid., 48.
24. Ibid.
25. "The Cause of Zion Today and Tomorrow" (Part One), in *Saints Herald* (August 1974): 10.
26. Ibid., 12.
27. Ibid., 13.
28. "The Cause of Zion Today and Tommorow" (Part Two), in *Saints Herald* (September 1974): 14–17.
29. Ibid., 26.
30. "On Being the Body of Christ," in *Saints Herald* (August 1976): 16.
31. Ibid., 17.

32. Ibid., 18.
33. Ibid., 29.
34. Ibid., 30.
35. "On Choosing Life" (Part One), in *Saints Herald* (November 1978): 16.
36. Ibid., 17.
37. Ibid.
38. Ibid., 37.
39. "On Choosing Life" (Part Two), in *Saints Herald* (December 1978): 16–17, 43.
40. Ibid., 43.
41. "Poised Between Eras," in *Saints Herald* (June 1, 1980): 6.
42. Ibid.
43. Ibid., 7.
44. Ibid., 8.
45. Ibid.
46. Ibid., 9.

■ CHAPTER 11 ■

The Prophetic View

Throughout his writings Clifford Cole applied the term "prophetic" not only in reference to one who exercised this responsibility as head of the church but also—and in the final analysis primarily—to a quality exhibited in the body of the church. In this connection, revelation was not so much contained in a document brought to the church at intervals by the presiding officer, as it was reflected in the response of the church to the mission to which God was calling it.

Virtually the first major work authored by Clifford, shortly after being assigned to the Department of Religious Education, sought to explore this quality as it was embodied in the Old Testament. This study was offered to counter the widely held view among Christians, including members of the RLDS Church, that prophecy dealt most significantly with the foretelling of future events, communicated by literally communicated messages from God. In many respects the book broke new ground for Latter Day Saints, encouraging both a closer acquaintance with and a deeper appreciation for those whose testimony was preserved in the Old Testament.

The Prophets Spoke

Clifford pointed out, first of all, that while a function of the prophet might be to discern the course of future events, this more accurately had to do with the *apocalyptic,* such as contained in the Revelation of Saint John and to some extent in the book of Daniel. Essentially, he wrote:

> [P]rophecy has to do with the revelation of the mind and will of God to men, and involves the future only as it bears upon God's purposes

for those to whom he speaks.... This occasionally has involved some unveiling of the future when God's purposes required it, but certainly such foretelling of future events has never been the major object of modern prophecy....[1]

Far from being some kind of automatic process in which humans received communications from God, the experience of revelation spoke of a struggle on the part of the prophet taken to the very edge of his capacity to understand, and then to communicate:

Every true prophet finds himself searching for words, expressions, symbols sometimes utilizing the power of song or drama to try to portray intelligibly the meaning and nature of his prophetic experience.... God seeks to reveal himself in terms of the background of experience and maturity of those to whom his message is directed. Nevertheless, we find ourselves stretching our spiritual and mental horizons to understand the meaning couched within his revelation.[2]

Against this background Clifford presented a more extensive and responsible review of the prophetic voices of the Old Testament than had customarily been available to members of the church. In describing the authorship of the books of the Mosaic Law, he referred to recent scholarship in proposing at least four sources for the Pentateuch in its present form, generally referred to as "J," "E," "P," and "D."[3] Here, as with other books of the Old Testament, Clifford encouraged readers to become familiar with the historical, cultural, and spiritual background of the people to whom the writings were addressed, in precisely the same way that contemporary church members would find their understanding of the Doctrine and Covenants enriched as they understood the background and circumstances of the documents.

Questions of precise accuracy in authorship were not so important to the ancient people as was the showing forth of the power of Jehovah, and the divine plan of redemption reflected in the events recorded. In some instances it was not possible to identify the writer(s) with any degree of certainty. A case in point would be the book of Daniel, written during the second century B.C. at the time of the revolt of the Maccabees:

> Primarily it was the author's purpose to encourage the people to remain true to God in the dark days when it looked as if Hebrew culture and the worship of Jehovah might be exterminated. The author chose an apocalyptic form of writing because he needed to veil its message in symbols which would not be understood by the Syrian conquerors.... The meaning was quite clear to the Hebrews of the day, however.... He placed the words in the mouth of Daniel who long since had died but whose heroic life during the days of the exile had earned a place for him among the Jewish heroes...[and] even though the meaning of much of Daniel is quite obscure, our appreciation for it increased when we read it in the light of the background out of which it developed.[4]

Clifford emphasized the importance of discerning the underlying historical and religious factors throughout the book. This was necessary to allow the text to point to the broader movement of God in the unfolding experience of the Hebrews. The prophets made their significant contribution not in foretelling the far-off future, but in forthtelling what God was calling the people to do in their current circumstances. It was unfortunate, in the writer's opinion, that the occasional bizarre incident in the text attracted so much curiosity that the more important message was virtually ignored:

> It is a sad commentary that our society has so often shown its littleness by quibbling over such incidental questions as "could a fish swallow a man?" or "how long could a man stay alive in a fish's belly?" These ar20 nos. 2 and 3):guments ought to be relegated to the heap of other absurdities.... Nobody ever thought to argue the point about whether or not Christ's parable of the good Samaritan actually happened. Nobody ever cared.[5]

Prophecy and Presidency

In 1972 when Clifford as director of Field Ministries addressed a gathering of stake presidents and bishops, he applied the concept of prophetic leadership to those in administrative roles in major jurisdictions of the church. While the content of the presentation was specifically directed to this group, the First Presidency considered that the principles stated were sufficiently important that they should be considered by those having responsibility in all jurisdictions of the church.

Clifford frankly acknowledged that the immediate past had been a time of painful reassessment, giving rise to divisions among the people, and even suspicion and lack of confidence. Moreover, he considered, "the problem is not over—there are more difficult times ahead." Against this background, he identified the administrative responsibilities of presiding officers:

> All of us are charged with the task of faithfully interpreting the objectives and programs of the world church to members as well as to those beyond the household of faith, and we have the obligation to solicit their support.... There is a place and a time for us to disagree.... But when decisions are made in the proper legislative or administrative bodies, and when we have exercised such appropriate rights of appeal as are provided for our protection and the protection of the church, then our integrity as leaders requires us to move forward, supporting the decisions made and the programs adopted by the church as long as we maintain our leadership role.[6]

Thus the demands of integrity, as well as the expectations of the leadership role, laid certain obligations on stake leaders. Yet beyond this supervisory function, there was a prophetic dimension to the ministry of leaders. It was in this respect that Clifford linked "presidency" and "prophecy":

> This means that you are much more than coordinators of a group of semi-autonomous congregat20 nos. 2 and 3):ions and departments....

> There is a sense in which the kind of accountability I have suggested here would indicate a primary concern with tightening discipline. While we must protect the church from those who would weaken and destroy it, our greater challenge—and indeed obligation—is to stand as affirmative and prophetic leaders to call the church to its mission and enable it to move forward. Presidency in the church is inevitably linked with prophecy, and in this sense I use the term to mean interpreting the mind and will of God both in word and in the tangible life of the body of the church.[7]

Such a response demanded a price, which we had not yet been prepared to pay. Turning to a theme that he was lifting up in other settings, Clifford identified the price of becoming prophetic, or the result of avoiding it:

> I believe that our greatest weakness is in our disposition to accept too uncritically the ideas and values and patterns of church life which have been inherited from former generations and also the values that are absorbed from the world around us.... Significantly we are told that it is the work and glory of God "to bring to pass the immortality and eternal life of man," and prophetic leadership must comprehend in some measure the meaning of that phrase and find ways to implement the program which has such a goal as its ultimate objective.[8]

Every leader was called to strengthen in his own life the needs that were held to be basic in the lives of the membership. These had to do with the strengthening of faith, which necessarily involved the ongoing testing of one's own beliefs in the climate of worship and prayer. This in turn called for the necessity of enabling learning "by study and also by faith" through creative programming:

> The prophetic need before us is not for innovative leadership but for creative leadership.... It requires freedom to think in new patterns but never requires change for change's sake alone. We must give attention to ways of leading our people into more satisfying experiences of worship which open their souls and lead them to wholeness and holiness. Our educational life must lead to deeper grappling with significant issues. People need help in the crucial areas of their lives.[9]

The prophetic administrator in the stake was supported by other leaders—the bishop, the high council—and ministered in such a way as to be close to the people, understanding their needs and enlisting their gifts. This was a major challenge that required all to be working together toward clearly perceived ends:

> We are charged with being administrators. In the church the administrator should be one of prophetic insight who has the ability to break the prophetic vision down into the steps necessary to take us from where we are to the goal we have set and then to have the ability to organize the resources at hand and inspire the people involved to achieve this goal.[10]

A Prophetic People

In another major *Saints Herald* presentation in 1975, Clifford extended these same principles to the life and ministry of the membership:

> It is the prophetic function to discern the nature of the world in which we live and call persons to look beyond the immediate to the eternal, out from the transient to the beckoning of God. It certainly would be unwise to curse the fluid character of our day. We are interested in change, for without it the kingdom of God can never be.... As a church, we are called to pay the price of being prophetic. Our mission is to sound the prophetic voice in a world that is amazingly dynamic, but torn by strife, often bewildered, prone to selfishness, terribly belligerent, and increasingly disillusioned.[11]

Clifford invited members to take a hard look at the demands implicit in such a prophetic calling. At the foundation was the need to know God through frequent prayer, study of the scriptures, and a sense of history. Such knowledge was not to be understood as an end in itself, but rather undertaken "so that we linked with the past and future in a profound awareness of responsibility to both." In this way scripture became a vehicle of revelation:

> We become in some measure prophetic when we abide in the climate and spirit of the prophets, and this is breathed into the Scriptures. For reasons not fully understood we are confronted by the Holy Spirit in a special way while reading the Scriptures—as if he hovers around them waiting for us to search them.[12]

The prophetic spirit was further nurtured by the spirit of praise and thanksgiving, expressed in the midst of the Saints. There was great strength in the community of the church, and members could draw prophetic strength from the body.

One dimension of the prophetic life was the readiness and discipline to open one's life to the eternal. The practical response was to understand the world in which that life was to be lived out in mission. Maintaining the analogy of the sea captain who concentrates on the ultimate at the expense of the immediate Clifford wrote the following:

> At the risk of oversimplifying the problem, I would suggest that the danger confronting a sea captain who concentrates on the time-proven reliability of the stars while ignoring the condition of this world has its counterpart in the kind of religiosity that concentrates on the unchangeability of God, the finality and literal authority of scripture, and the insistence on re-creating and freezing society in the mold of some past era to the neglect or disparagement of study and appreciation of this world.[13]

Most religious bodies were sometimes distracted by people who, unable or unwilling to pursue honest and serious study, claimed to possess "superior knowledge gleaned from the hidden meanings of the scriptures or some mystical experience" to which others were meant to give unthinking assent.

> While the Restoration movement has not been free from such prophets, it has always maintained a theological stance opposed to them. We are commanded to seek "out of the best books words of wisdom; seek learning even by study, and also by faith."[14]

Recalling the Statement of Objectives first announced in 1966 calling the church to discern the "signs of the times," Clifford issued once again the challenge to the church:

> If we are to be prophetic we must pay the price to understand the world in which we are cast. We must discern the signs of the times, and with a deep appreciation and love for that world speak to it in its own language and in the spirit of the reconciling love of God. The attitude of exclusiveness which would cause us to remain aloof and untainted will render us ineffective as leaders in a world God is trying to save.... To identify with the world means to love it and suffer with it and undeservedly carry its shame as Christ carries ours.[15]

The principles of the Sermon on the Mount, in Clifford's view, contained as sound a blueprint for facing the "New World" as might be found. Referring to the claims of some to possess the final answer to humankind's need, he wrote:

> I do not believe we have a plan for restructuring the world in spite of all the inspired instruction given us since 1820, nor do I think that it is possible for a divine plan to be given at one time in one place which is the correct model for all times and all cultures.... [W]e must be fully immersed in a sense of Scripture and history, but we must not be bound to it as if our salvation could be achieved by recapturing the past.[16]

With full faith in God and in the Holy Spirit as the active agent in remaking both individuals and the church as a whole, the Saints would find themselves developing the capacity to have faith in the people of the world, as the locus of God's loving and saving action. To participate in that world would call us to be a wise and learned people, understanding our times in depth and knowing that our strength was ultimately the strength of the whole church as the body of Christ. In summary:

> We must live and work in hope. We minister as a church in a world where the risks are great but where as a prophetic people of courage we call all mankind to the light, knowing that as many as will are called to be agents of reconciliation and love.... Further, as agents

of God's power we shall not have the kingdom for ourselves unless we can enable the kingdom to come to the world. This is our calling in mission. It is this burden that is laid on all of us to be a prophetic people in mission today.[17]

Notes

1. *The Prophets Speak* (Herald House, 1954), 9–10.
2. Ibid., 10–11.
3. Ibid., 17.
4. Ibid., 189–190.
5. Ibid., 180.
6. "Prophetic Leadership—A Continuing Need" (Part One), in *Saints Herald* (November 1972): 10.
7. Ibid., 11.
8. Ibid.
9. Ibid., 12.
10. "Prophetic Leadership—A Continuing Need" (Part Two), in *Saints Herald* (December 1972): 15.
11. "The Prophetic Voice, Called to Mission" (Part One), in *Saints Herald* (December 1975): 16–17.
12. Ibid.
13. Ibid., 18.
14. Ibid.
15. "The Prophetic Voice, Called to Mission" (Part Two), in *Saints Herald* (January 1976): 14.
16. Ibid., 15.
17. Ibid., 28.

■ CHAPTER 12 ■

In Retrospect

The following is a statement by Clifford Cole reviewing the development of the church during the period of his active appointment, As proposed earlier in this study, these were years of critical experience for the church, a time when divisions among the membership over fundamental issues began to be evident. Clifford's voice, as recognized in the document granting him honorable release from the Council of Twelve, brought a "calming spirit and reasoned approach" to the explorations that were setting the course for the future. In retrospect, Clifford writes as follows:

Some developments took place during the years of our active church appointment that gave me genuine hope for the future of the church. Among these are five areas of growth, which took place under what I consider to be a powerful and widely shared prophetic direction of the Holy Spirit. If these developments had not taken place, we would never have become a world church.

1. During that period we moved from a church of exclusiveness to a church that recognized we are part of a much larger Christian world. God is at work with and through us but God is working through many organizations as well. The church I grew up in as a boy took great pride in proclaiming that the RLDS Church was the only true church recognized by God. We reasoned that the church through the "Dark Ages" of the past had departed so completely from the church originally established by Christ and the apostles that God withdrew his church from the earth. We referred to this as the Apostasy. Hence there was no true

Christian church when Joseph Smith by the power of God restored his church again in the world. This proved to the satisfaction of the RLDS membership that when God restored the church through Joseph Smith it was the only true church with authority from God.

This line of thinking was not original with us. It had come down through the Anabaptist movement which emerged from Zurich, Switzerland, and was later transported to the American colonies. These "restoration" groups took the position that the Apostasy had left the church so devastated that it could not be reformed by people but would need to be divinely restored to its original state as Christ had established it. That belief became the center of our missionary message, and convincing people of that belief was the reason for the existence of the church.

Through the time of our appointee ministry, however, some perplexing questions began to emerge. Theologically, many asked, "How could Christ's church arise out of such a complete apostasy unless Christ was born among us, grew up, and established the church again?" It was clear that all Christian churches were grounded in our common memory of Christ's ministry as recorded in the Bible. Forms of worship and traditions passed from generation to generation, and our faith in God and Christ was rooted in our common Christian history. Although we had enriched and added to our understanding of the gospel through the Book of Mormon and Doctrine and Covenants, we were still a Christian church standing on foundations of the Christian faith from the days of Christ and the early Christian Church.

2. We based much of our exclusiveness on our experience with continued revelation. This was brought to us by the one sustained as prophet and also as we experienced the gifts of the Spirit in worship. Many converts, however, had experienced the Holy Spirit in worship in other denominations and stated that we were being very arrogant and, in

fact, wrong in claiming that God was exclusively with the RLDS Church. They had been blessed by the Spirit while they were members of other denominations. They were at times disturbed by the misuse of the so-called "gifts of the Spirit" and began raising questions about our use of such gifts.

We were very proud in our belief and experience in "continued revelation." The validity of our claim that continuing revelation was a distinctive within the RLDS Church and the embarrassment of its misuse has led us to more thoughtful consideration of its role in the church. This evaluation has raised questions about our use of scripture, such as the Bible, the Book of Mormon, and the Doctrine and Covenants. More and more these scriptures are seen as the results of our human struggle to understand and experience God's presence in our midst. However, they are not plenary. They are the result of the amalgamation of our humanity, with all its cultural limitations, preconceived beliefs, and human desires as it is impacted by God through the Holy Spirit, and especially through his Only Begotten Son, Jesus Christ. Scriptures are not absolute.

3. Our concept of authority has changed during the years under consideration. In the early RLDS Church the Apostasy was seen more or less as an event in which God withdrew from humans the authority to represent the divine will on earth. Therefore the "restoration" of authority was also part of God's act of restoring to mankind the right to represent him on earth. It was our belief that divine authority had to be given to the church through Joseph Smith, and no other denomination had the right to represent God. Priesthood was the channel through which divine power flowed to God's people. It was assumed that these priesthood members would be godly men free from "worldly vices" such as adultery, fornication, stealing, lying, cursing, drinking alcoholic liquors, using tobacco, or other sinful acts. Affir-

matively they should be diligent in ministry, honest financial stewards supportive of the church and its beliefs, dedicated to Christ, and sacrificially committed to exemplary Christian values.

Questions arose among the membership when it was discovered that some priesthood men were not living that high quality of life and had been doing so even before they were called and ordained. Some claiming divine authority broke away from the parent church, subsequently leading a dissident movement and claiming that they spoke for God. Such actions caused deep divisions in some congregations and concerns about the basis of the church's authority.

Furthermore, the attitude has developed that RLDS priesthood has authority granted by the RLDS Church, but that other denominations also grant their officials and ministers similar powers to function within their organization. We ought not to be so arrogant as to assume that God only works within and through the RLDS Church. The question of whom God recognizes is not determined by us, but rather by God. Therefore we ought to accept the fact that God is working in many places and many ways to fulfill the divine purposes in the world. We should not disparage the good ministry of others but rather concentrate on our own calling and mission for Jesus Christ. Authority is more related to how adequate and faithful we are to our discipleship than to some outwardly bestowed right.

4. We have moved from the position of claiming that our purpose for existing is to proclaim our "distinctives" from other Christian churches. Our mission is to proclaim Jesus Christ as the Only Begotten Son of God above all else. Two developments have brought this calling pointedly to our attention. One was the ferment that developed, especially during the 1950s and 1960s among the youth of major nations of the world. When confronted by our long-time message of being distinctive from other Christian denomi-

nations, many responded by saying, "I'm not much interested in your distinctives. I feel that the bickering of the church with other Christian denominations only raises the question as to whether or not *any* church is seriously concerned about the crucial issues the world is confronting. What are you saying or doing about war, nuclear weapons, world overpopulation, poverty, disease, and starvation? We think life on this planet may end before we have lived out our lives, but no church seems to speak to these issues. Do you think God is not concerned about such things?"

The other development was the expansion of the RLDS Church into the non-Christian societies of the world. The RLDS Church appointees who were assigned to Japan, Korea, India, and other nations where Christianity was little known began writing to church officials at headquarters pleading for materials and assistance for missionary outreach in the non-Christian societies. These missionaries were saying to us: "All of the literature, audio-visual materials and other missionary helps have to do with the ways the RLDS Church is different from other Christian denominations. People here do not want to know the differences existing among us Christians. They want to know what the basic Christian beliefs are." This caused us to understand that our desire to become a world church would lead us to reevaluate our message.

We at the World Church headquarters recognized that our missionary message had been developed in a negative way against other denominations but that the very fundamental beliefs about God, Jesus Christ, the common call to discipleship, had not been a part of our proclamation of the gospel. As this understanding began to influence the church school curriculum, missionary message, and worship programs, there was a serious dissident movement that developed within the church. In the face of this, those of us who were in responsible positions of leadership concluded that the church could not fulfill its divine mission to be a world church unless we moved forward to teach the whole gospel without regard to what any other movement was teaching. We must not neglect to teach the basic faith because other denominations taught it also. In fact, it became clear that we were being helped by other churches as they joined with us in teaching those beliefs that were true and shared by all Christians.

5. We had moved from a concept of Zion as an exclusive, isolated, self-sustaining, theocratic conclave to seeing Zion as a basic fellowship which is a leaven in the world but not separated from it. The New England colonies which nurtured the ancestors of Joseph Smith were settled by Europeans who came to America hoping to establish more perfect societies free from the governmental restrictions of European nations and the evil influence of their worldly neighbors. This led to the conviction that such settlements should be composed exclusively of people of similar beliefs, commitments, and allegiances. They were to be rooted in scriptural and divinely given patterns. They were to be model societies that other peoples of the world would emulate, and because they were called to a divine destiny, their victory was sure. Those who opposed them were eventually to be defeated by their own wickedness and greed. For the RLDS, the place for this to happen was Jackson County and regions round about. Most RLDS Church members expected that the time would soon arrive when the First Presidency and Presiding Bishopric would issue the call for the RLDS membership to gather to the central area to "build Zion." This was considered to be the place of safety for the Saints.

Tremendous changes were brought about by the two world wars and by scientific developments in technology, travel, and communications. These pressed the whole world into one great community where isolation was no longer possible. Hence a great reorientation took place inside and outside the RLDS Church membership. When the church expanded into many nations of the world it found that other cultures of the world did not want to be Americanized and, in fact, ought not to be. We began to realize that we were not called as Christians to transplant American colonies around the world, nor was it possible to gather our converts to a gathering place in America.

In the period of the 1960s and 1970s we came to understand that our mission was to be the spiritual social leaven that could transform other cultures. We needed to develop leaders in each culture who could interpret the deeper principles of Christian life in terms of the cultural climate of the country. The Zionic mission of the church was seen not as a specific economic and social set of procedures but rather as the universal call for Christians to live in communities and support each other in expressing the gospel of Christ in their everyday activities.

I personally take great satisfaction in having been permitted to be involved with other brothers and sisters in working through the five developments mentioned above. Without these the RLDS Church could not have become a successful world organization. Furthermore, these developments laid the groundwork for growth that has taken place since my retirement. That growth will continue on into the future. The principle of continued divine revelation assures us that no one period of time will be frozen and preserved as the everlasting perfect society. We must always be growing, for that is the nature of God's creative plan.

CHAPTER 13

In Appreciation

Author's Note

During the last twenty-two years of his assignment as a World Church appointee, Clifford served as a member of the Council of Twelve, the last sixteen of these as president of the council. This responsibility brought him into contact with other general officers in a close collegial relationship. A number of these colleagues have been asked to make a statement of appreciation of Clifford's friendship and leadership in the roles he was called to fulfill. Each of those approached was more than happy to make such a statement. They follow here.

Duane E. Couey:

One of the most meaningful friendships and collegial relationships I have ever experienced came in the years I was associated with Clifford Cole as I worked with him when I was in the First Presidency. Clifford was one of the leaders of that period who was qualified by advanced education and insight into the matter of where the church really was at that time. He entered the Council of Twelve in 1958 along with another amazing minister, Charles Neff, who also came to be one of the leaders of that period.

Clifford and I were assigned neighboring offices in the old Council of Twelve suite on Level 2 of the Auditorium. The proximity of location and the mutual interests we seemed to share provided the basis for many long conversations, most of them having to do with history and theology. I had little theological education at that point, but I experienced a growing hunger for it. As an appointee I had served in a number of assignments: missionary, stake and district administrator, and in various other assignments. I lacked the systematic education that Clifford had attained and used so well, but he always encouraged me and never diminished any possible contribution I could make.

As time went on I found myself in growing admiration of Clifford Cole and men like him. At that time there was developing in the Council of Twelve a real sense of mission. New faces with new experiences, including those from the recently concluded World War II, were beginning to raise a whole series of questions about the church and its mission.

It was also the time when the entry of the church into non-Western areas and mounting societal changes in the West were making their demands on the church and especially on its leaders. At this juncture in my experience I readily displayed my highly conservative background, which served me well in earlier years when the church was different from what it had become. During this time, long conversations with Clifford and others along with the phrasing of strategic questions made me realize how poorly prepared I was to be a leader for that time.

Because Clifford was such a discerning person he was fully aware of what was happening in me and always gave me great support and encouragement. There were never any unjust demands on me either intellectually or in any other way. He was always an understanding friend, giving wise counsel on which I could depend and trust.

I well remember when Clifford was selected to be president of the Twelve in 1964. Meeting in the old council chamber in the Auditorium, the council decided that there would be no nominations received, but rather a series of ballots cast until someone received a majority. From four names offered on the first ballot, Clifford eventually emerged as president. Although I had supported Charles Neff, the eventual decision was one that I never regretted, because it became clear to me that both of these men were persons of destiny. President W. Wallace Smith had demonstrated his profound insight in calling both of these men to join the ranks of general officers as one of his very first actions in 1958.

As the pages of our history are opened to that time I am almost overwhelmed by the amazing things that happened. My oral history memoir calls but a few of those remarkable developments to mind. The Twelve began to move with a common vision over the next few years, when we began to see Clifford's remarkable leadership skills in action. He was always the "apostle," his words, sayings, and stories rooted in his testimony of the Christ.

With the development of the church objectives in 1966, the First Presidency was fully in support of the vision that had gradually emerged. The period that followed saw times of difficulty but Clifford never wavered in his commitment to see a different role for the church in the future. It was my privilege to travel throughout the world with Clifford during my years in the First Presidency. Through this experience I became aware of his ability to relate to many kinds of people.

One thing about Clifford that I will always remember is that when assignments were changed he did not reluctantly go to new duties. He would immediately turn his attention to the new role.

Clifford was very sensitive to my needs during the period of the illness and death of my first wife, Edith. His compassion will always be a memory of blessing.

Brother Cole and I have always remained close. We would often meet for lunch and discuss what was closest to our hearts. One day, after we were preparing to leave such a discussion, the Spirit came to me in great power. The words that came to me were: "I have never been with you that I did not receive a blessing of ministry." And it was the truth.

My life is infinitely richer because of Clifford A. Cole. He helped me to believe in myself as well as to believe and trust in God. He will always reside in my memory clearly in all of his special and unique abilities. Few people could have had the rare privilege of the close association we enjoyed together over those years and which we still mark as some of the most significant years of our lives. I thank him for all that he is and all that he has been.

J. C. Stuart:

It was in Lamoni, Iowa, on a hot, dusty afternoon late in August 1934 that I first met Clifford Cole. I greeted him as he climbed down from the bus. He was an incoming freshman at Graceland College. I was a returning student appointed to meet the bus and welcome newcomers to the college.

To me he looked like I thought he should, coming from the wide open plains of Wyoming—a sort of green, awkward farm boy. My being a city boy from Los Angeles might have affected the way I viewed him. If someone had told me he would later serve as dean at the college, then as an apostle for the church, and a little later as president of the Council of Twelve Apostles, I would have said, "No way!"

It was twenty-four years later that Clifford Cole, as a new apostle for the church, came to Ontario to become acquainted with the London District where I served as district president and London city pastor. As we traveled together by car I kept asking him difficult questions. I think he probably knew I was testing him. At the close of the day I came home and told my wife, Eleanor: "The new apostle is OK. I think he's going to make it." He had neither avoided my questions nor did he try to impress me with his wisdom.

It was some years later when he was president of the Council of Twelve and I was a member of the council that I saw him function in that significant presiding role. He was always calm, well-organized, and straightforward.

Clifford had the remarkable ability to identify clearly the nature of the issues to be discussed and their ramifications. His sound and reasoned approach to the business coming before the council kept the discussion on a high level and helped avoid clashes that could have occurred when strong-minded people had differing opinions.

Two other qualities that were so naturally a part of his personality did much to smooth the way for dealing with difficult issues. First, he had a keen sense of humor—a sort of dry wit—that at times brought us down to earth when discussions became heavy and intense. Also, he was a great storyteller. It was a delight to hear him tell of humorous incidents that touched on our human foibles. I can recall how, in the midst of strong and heated debate, he would at times interrupt the discussion by saying something like "This reminds me of the farmer who had two cows...." Everybody would lean back, relax, and listen with keen anticipation. At the end of the story we were able to continue discussion in a more rational manner.

Clifford and I were born in the same year. I was born in August, he in November. I once told him that I would respect him because he was my superior officer, but that he needed to respect me because I was his senior. Each November he would smile and say to me: "J.C., I don't need to respect you until next August." Such was the jovial expression of a kind and dedicated man graced with a keen mind and a delightful sense of humor.

I think the good Lord must have smiled when he created Clifford.

Alan D. Tyree:

My first contact with Clifford occurred at a Nauvoo youth camp when he was a rather young camp director and I was a teenage junior counselor. I don't remember many of the things that happened that week, but I recall that another junior counselor and I—we were college students at the time—went for a drive in his car one afternoon early in the week, without seeking the director's permission to leave the grounds. I was immature enough to be unaware that there were good reasons why we should ask for permission. In a gentle but unquestionably firm way Clifford gave appropriate counsel to us about our responsibilities. I cannot say that the incident particularly endeared Clifford to me, or me to him, but it did gain my respect for him and his leadership qualities. Ever since, I have recognized him as a dependable and respectful administrator who always worked within the framework of a pastoral relationship.

Years later I was privileged to serve as a member of the Council of Twelve while he was its president. My admiration and appreciation grew and expanded the longer we served together. The original qualities and gifts he had shown in earlier years matured into an excellent leadership that brought many blessings to the church. He was one of the key persons who created a climate of service that permitted the entire council—and by extension the Joint Council of First Presidency, Twelve, and Bishopric as well—to labor together unitedly without the feelings of division that had existed earlier in the church's experience.

Illustrative of that unity is the way we became accustomed to the practice of moving to reconsider an action whenever the vote was close. It was indicative of our desire for togetherness in our work. If we needed more time to consider and discuss the issue in order to achieve that togetherness, then we wanted to treat those who had not come to the majority point of view with a respect that permitted them to reason their way through the issues at stake. Eventually, and usually soon, we came to a unity that permitted us all to be supportive of the action taken by the council, and we could leave for our fields of ministry knowing that there was mutual support among us all. I do not recall Clifford ever acting in such a manner that anyone was caused to do something they did not want to do, nor did he need to take strong administrative action causing hurt to anyone. The council followed his leadership in its actions as well.

Clifford was the first president of the Council of Twelve to be chosen, not by seniority, but by nomination and election without consideration of seniority. The Council of Twelve elected him upon wise direction from the president of the church, and that pattern of nomination and election has followed ever since. He was also the first director of Field Ministries. Serving in that role while he was also president of the council placed a great deal of authority in his hands. Until his designation, the individual apostles had exercised rather complete autonomy over the assigned fields of ministerial labor. Clifford carefully and meticulously served in these dual capacities without causing the individual field apostles to sense any loss of personal authority and responsibility. It was a delicate role, and he created the pattern for those who were to follow him.

One of the endearing traits for which we appreciated him most was his sense of humor. He could tell homespun stories that would cause both laughter and comprehension. Frequently his stories illuminated a matter so that consensus was easily reached. One story—which I can only poorly retell—was about two hunters, camping in the wilderness. They hoped to bring back some major game, perhaps even a bear. One of them remained in camp, preparing dinner, while the other set out to do a bit of hunting. He found his bear all right, but the bear surprised him and he had to run for his life. As he tore back into camp, not wanting to admit the predicament he had gotten himself into, he shouted to his friend as he ran through their tent: "Here, you prepare this one, and I'll go back and get another!"

Clifford recounted this story to us more than once when some of the council members, in our zeal to advance the cause of the gospel, had a tendency to want to do too much too soon. He was suggesting that there might be a bear in the wilderness, waiting to surprise us in unanticipated ways. We should not set goals that were too numerous or too far-reaching, but exercise the careful preparation and precautionary planning necessary to our common endeavor.

As a writer, teacher, preacher, leader, pastor, and mentor, Clifford has been a valued friend and colleague to whom I, and the church, owe a great debt of gratitude.

Maurice L. Draper:

In terms of personality and character Clifford Cole can best be described as a "gentleman's gentleman." In all of our relationships he always demonstrated a rare combination of gentleness and courage. Not only was this true in the process of daily routines when there were decisions to be made calling for adjustments in procedure and definition of programs and assignments, but it was a great blessing to his colleagues in formal settings.

During official meetings of the presiding officers in "joint council," situations sometimes arose in which there were alternative interpretations in the debate about significant issues. Many times Clifford listened carefully to these discussions before making his contribution. Then he would skillfully and briefly summarize the important elements as he understood them in such a spirit that his conclusions seemed to many of us to be what we had been talking about all the time. His contributions never sounded like arguments but as clarifications by which each one was helped to recognize our common understanding.

As time passed this quality became a personal resource to some other members of the presiding quorums. In this process several of us were developing a similar orientation to our work as general officers. This was particularly true of Clifford, Charles Neff, Duane Couey, and myself. The difference in personality traits, gifts, and interests seemed to blend in ways that, speaking for myself at least, have been enriching to each of us.

At lunch we frequently discussed some aspects of church administration, theological and doctrinal questions, the content and meaning of our own church history, personnel needs, and sometimes factors in our own ministerial responsibilities. For me these discussions were both stimulating and supportive. I do not recall a single instance in which Clifford's expressions, whether in council sessions or our personal interactions, were less than helpful. Indeed, we seemed to grow in spiritual intimacy and broadening arena of intellectual understanding. Clifford's penetrating insight and kindly responses were invaluable.

Donald V. Lents:

My appraisal of Clifford A. Cole is that he has always been a man open and willing to listen to all points of view, a friend to be trusted, considerate and honest in all his relationships.

Over a period of many years and the varied activities of our ministry our association was always a rich and rewarding experience for me. During his tenure as president of the Council of Twelve I had the privilege of serving as secretary, which brought us into a close working relationship. At all times I found him to be compassionate and fair, truly a man of integrity as the council worked together for the benefit of the people of the church and in developing consensus concerning the call of the Lord to our responsibilities and opportunities.

A particular memory concerning Clifford's leadership comes to my mind that clearly highlights the quality of his concern for integrity and fairness. Several times during the period I served as secretary it was not possible for me to attend council sessions because of assignments and commitments in missions abroad. There were issues of concern on which Clifford and I had different opinions and approaches as to the best way to bring ministry in specific situations. Other members of the council informed me on my return that Clifford was very careful and concerned that where our ideas differed my voice should be heard. His procedure was that during their discussions and before voting, Brother Clifford would share an observation like this: "Brethren, Brother Lents is not present to share his view, but if he were here, I believe he would call our attention to these two or three points." Even on those occasions when our positions and feelings might be in opposition to each other, he wanted in fairness to be certain all voices were being heard. Such character and integrity was an integral part of Brother Cole's leadership style.

It was a privilege to have been permitted to receive his calming ministry on a number of occasions. Lives are enhanced and enriched in friendship of deep, heartfelt association, and I am blessed with the appreciation of rich fellowship and companionship with Clifford Cole, my fellow worker and brother in a faith that has made this possible.

Reed M. Holmes:

Clifford Cole was an exceptional person who never lost the common touch. Being a shepherd in the hills of Wyoming had something to do with his responsible, caring ministry, and it was good training for the future apostle.

Whether Clifford was speaking from the pulpit or writing church school materials he was never "highfalutin." His insights were penetrating, but of what value would they be if they did not strike a responsive chord? And so his words have always been alive, drawing pictures we can see and understand.

We all have a number of friends we love with all our hearts. I have found that loving one child or grandchild with all my heart did not diminish my love for each of the others. Just so, Clifford has been my very best friend, along with Don and Maurice and Abrahama, and a few others.

Our friendship grew in quiet sharing in regard to the church's need of a sound curriculum; also, in probing discussions with a diversity of loyal minds on the Basic Beliefs Committee as we sought a clear, but never final statement of the church's faith exploration. Coming to consensus is rarely easy. To balance personal certainty with openness to developing insights from others is a challenge, but with Clifford around, the wisdom of both mind and heart comes through.

We shared times of relaxation as well. Once in a while we were "gone fishin'." It was a time to share with our sons, Larry and David. We also went fishing with W. Wallace Smith and shared amusement when Wallace went thrashing with his fishing pole after the fish he brought up to the boat refused to come aboard!

Clifford has the ability to calm the troubled soul. I've witnessed this in time of serious crisis, but also remembered him calming my troubled soul when, in Tahiti, I stuck my foot in a shoe already occupied by a centipede more than six inches long, a good six inches wide, and sporting pinchers on its business end.

Seriously, the steadying, friendly support of Clifford Cole has been a strength. Always slow to chide and quick to encourage, Clifford is one who, I am sure, brings a smile to another Good Shepherd.

Howard S. Sheehy Jr.:

In order to respond to an urgent and unexpected need at Graceland College, Clifford Cole, at the request of the Board of Trustees, was assigned by the Joint Council from his church work in western Iowa to serve as dean of students in September 1951. His one-year assignment was continued for an additional year, and in that manner Clifford Cole was the dean of students for both of my years at Graceland College. In addition to his administrative duties he also taught some classes. I was his student in a psychology lab and in Sociology 101 my first year. During my sophomore year I worked as a "faculty assistant" to Clifford in one of his multiple roles as director of Religious Life. Essentially I organized the order of worship and participants for the campus religious program. My first and early association with Clifford was very satisfying: he was a friend, and quiet mentor who encouraged me to be creative and energetic in fulfilling my responsibilities.

At the end of the year I asked him to write in my yearbook, the 1953 *Acacia*. He wrote:

Dear Howard,
    During the past year we have had many experiences that we shall treasure as long as we live. Words that I write here will never express the appreciation which I feel for the fellowship I have had with you, but trust that some of the experiences will in themselves let you know how much I have come to think of you. Through the years ahead I am looking forward to you joining continuously in the

work of the church in a way that will keep us working together for a long time. /s/ *Clifford Cole*

I continued on with my college career and Clifford returned to World Church appointment as the director of Religious Education at church headquarters. While at Graceland my future wife, Florine, was especially impressed by Clifford's "servant ministry" when, during an "influenza epidemic" that sent the college nurse and infirmary staff to their beds, she found Clifford washing the dishes in the infirmary kitchen to meet the need of the day. When we set a date for our wedding two years later we agreed that the minister for our wedding would be the "Dean of Students," who was willing to wash the dishes. I found that anecdotal experience to be a deep-rooted characteristic of Clifford.

Clifford was the president of the Council of Twelve the entire time I served in the council. While our relationship was not one of dean and student, I continued to experience a very constructive and supportive climate that pressed me to be fully responsible for decisions in my field of assignment. At the same time, he was always open to listening to my concerns and encouraging my efforts to grow. His ability to give me space and time to develop was a blessing.

His gracious and genuine testimony to me when I accepted the call to serve as a member of the First Presidency was typical of our lifelong relationship. There was always the climate for personal development and role model of excellence in ministry and humility of spirit that is characteristic of spiritual leaders and true friends. My life, and the life of the church, have been deeply enriched by his application of very capable teaching skills.

Lloyd B. Hurshman:

The vast prairies of northeastern Wyoming stretch the horizons of mind and soul. This vastness seeped into my consciousness while driving north from Colorado shortly after the World Conference of 1976 to the home of District President Aubrey "Chub" Long and his wife, Alice, in Alva. Regional Administrator Lewis Landsberg was introducing me to leaders and members in part of my new Council of Twelve field assignment.

While visiting after dinner, we studied the locations of district congregations on a map of Wyoming. I remembered Clifford's classes and sermons being enriched by illustrations of growing up, tending flocks, teaching school, and keeping store at a place called Oshoto, lying west of Alva. I was aware that the Cole family and other homesteading families had built a church and worshiped at a prairie site nearby. At my request, "Chub" pointed to an unmarked place on the map where the Oshoto church once stood. Lacking any perspective of the distances involved, I asked "Chub" if it were possible to drive to the Oshoto church during our free time before meeting leaders and members the next day. "Chub" nodded yes without hesitation.

A tiny hint of what lay to the west occurred as I walked toward my church car the next morning. "Chub" suggested gently that it might be wise to take his four-wheel-drive pickup truck instead. We drove west on excellent highway, but eventually "Chub" turned onto a gravel road, then a dirt track, and finally pointed the truck straight west across rolling grasslands.

As we stood by the ruins of the church, I looked to distant horizons in all directions. In those precious moments, I gained a greatly enlarged perspective of the surroundings that had helped form and stretch the soul and mind of Clifford Cole, this man who had widened my horizons whenever and wherever we met—as dean of students at Graceland College, through ministry in various congregations and wider gatherings, as spokesperson for my ordination to the high priesthood, and now as president of the Twelve.

Along with other personal heroes who have helped open my mind and soul to wider horizons of the divine creation, I will always be grateful for Clifford's clear, fresh insights in spoken and written word, for his ability to build healing bridges across seemingly irreconcilable chasms of opinion, for his rich humor, for his compassionate personal ministries.

Another insight has come to me as I have contemplated the restless, wind-starved grasses of those great prairies. Clifford's calm demeanor and reasoned views cloak a restless passion for the far horizons of truth, for righteousness, justice, and mercy.

■ APPENDIX ■

A Parable of Mission*

I dreamed, and in my dream a man from the Orient stood before me. He was neatly dressed and held in his hand the Three Standard Books.

"I have come to help you," he said.

"Fine," I replied. "We can surely use help. Perhaps we can go down to the stake office in the morning and get a checkup on your skills to see where you could make the best contribution here."

"Oh, no," my visitor countered. "The church in Japan sent me here. We have a program which I shall be directing, but I would like to meet with the leaders to see who might be best qualified to help us."

"I see. In that event I need to know more about your program," I shot back.

"Since we have become members of Christ's Church," said the man, "we have felt a desire to help all people enjoy the blessings we have. In Japan we have been terribly concerned about the breakdown in American family life. God has blessed our nation greatly in this respect. In fact, our family life in many respects parallels the family patterns of Old Testament Hebrew times. In the spirit of the Restoration movement we feel called to help the peoples of the world recapture the stable family relationships which God established in ancient days. We call this project 'Into All the World.'"

"How do you plan to work in America?" I said.

---

*From "The Church in Culture," in the *Saints Herald* (June 1977): 43–44. The parable needs no further explanation.

"We have been preparing for this," he said. "We have selected materials about our family life and history and the reverence we pay to the elderly. Of course we will have a big job translating them into English. We have been concerned because we have noted quite a few of our illustrations don't seem to mean much to Americans, and our philosophy seems hard for you to grasp. There just aren't English words to express the right meanings, and Americans aren't capable of the thought patterns we have.

"We do have a dandy film, though. It shows opening scenes of the beauty and peace and inner-family support in Japanese homes. But the bulk of the film, highlighting the problems, was made in America. Shots made in the schools show the effect of broken homes on children, especially those in classes for the emotionally disturbed and hyperactive children. We have several minutes of film from divorce courts and a review of this awful 'no fault' divorce law so many of your states have. Our best footage, though, is made in your homes for the aged. Our people were really moved by the terrible conditions and isolation of the elderly in America. We can't even imagine being left in old age with no family to care for us. That film has really given the church in Japan a boost."

"Well," I said, with more than a little irritation, "what do you expect to do here to solve all those problems?"

"We are going to convert families to the Japanese structure. We will need to set up a community," he stated. "Of course, we will raise money in Japan to get the community started."

"But American families don't live together in that kind of durable community life," I countered, "and our houses aren't made for that kind of extended family. In fact, the average family—which is made up of husband, wife, and children still at home—moves every three years."

"That's the reason we need money from Japan to set this

project up," he said. "We know we will have to subsidize this to make it work."

"But your community will be artificial to our culture," I argued. "Our people work for big corporations that move them around from city to city and sometimes outside the country. Our women work outside the home, and they are not going to fit into the husband-mother-in-law dominated family life you want to promote."

"They will if they are truly converted to Christ," replied my guest. "The family unit is basic to developing lives of worth and achieving eternal life."

"Well, don't you think we had better talk this over with the stake president and see how he would feel about setting it up?" I asked.

"You don't seem to understand," said the man from the Orient. "The Saints in Japan are raising a lot of money for this. They're not going to turn over such an important project to someone else, especially in a country where practically no one would understand the kind of family we are trying to produce. Besides, the corporation that is looking for land to buy has its own bylaws and policies."

"Why don't you just stay in Japan," I suggested, "and concentrate on being the church there? I guess God still knows where we are and can help us work out our problems here."

BIBLIOGRAPHY

Books and Articles in Other Publications
The Prophets Speak (Herald House, 1954).
Faith for New Frontiers (Herald House, 1956).
The Revelation in Christ (Herald House, 1963).
Distinctives Yesterday and Today, co-authored with Peter Judd (Herald House, 1983).
The Mighty Acts of God (Herald House, 1984).
The Priesthood Manual (Herald House, revisions 1982 and 1985).
Studies in Exodus, Vols. 1 and 2 (Herald House, 1986).
Jesus the Christ (senior high study text for Department of Religious Education, 1961–1962).
This Is My Father's World co-authored with Gwen Amsberry (primary teacher's manual for Department of Religious Education, 1955).
Modern Women in a Modern World (Department of Women, 1985).
Working Together in Our Families (Family Living Series for Department of Women, 1955).
Celebrating Together in Our Families (Family Living Series for Department of Women, 1955).
"Our Mission in Light of Today's Demands" in *Zion Building*, edited by Richard Hughes (reunion study text for adults and youth, 1978).
"The Nature of God" in *Facing Today's Frontiers* (Department of Religious Education, 1965).

ced*Saints Herald:* General Articles
"The Unfinished Furrow" (April 7, 1952): 5.
"A Morality for Our Day" (December 6, 1954): 5.

"Women in a Witnessing Fellowship" (December 22, 1958): 12.
"Measured by the Heart" (November 21, 1960): 4.
"Role of the Critic in the Church" (July 1, 1962): 462.
"The Restoration Is Universal" (November 1, 1962): 9.
"New Joys from an Old Task" (September 15, 1963): 6.
"A More Excellent Way" (October 1, 1963): 8.
"The Branch Looks at Its Calling" (November 1, 1963): 10.
"The Meaning of Zion in Our time" (May 15, 1968): 10.
"The Church Is Interested in Marriage" (November 1969): 10.
"Family Festivals and Holidays" (December 1969): 13.
"Theological Perspectives of World Mission," an address given at the Conference of High Priests and Seventies (July 1971: 10; chosen for the Elbert A. Smith Memorial Award in 1971).
"Prophetic Leadership: A Continuing Need" (November 1972): 10; and (December 1972): 15.
"Expressions of the Holy Spirit" (January 1975): 10.
"The Prophetic Voice: Called to Mission" (December 1975): 16; and (January 1976): 14.
"The Church in Culture," dialogue with Alan D. Tyree (March 1976): 12.
"Theological Issues Confronting Older Youth Today" (September 1976): 6.
"The Church in Culture" (June 1977): 12; excerpted from an address given at a Zionic Research Institute workshop in August 1975.
"Explorations in Becoming a World Church" (August 1978): 19.
"An Apostle Looks at Thanksgiving" (November 1978): 6.
"The Right and Wrong of Dissent" (May 1979): 6.
"Last of All" (December 1979): 7.

"The Best Gift" (April 1984): 12.
"Reflections on W. Wallace Smith" (October 1989): 5.

Saints Herald: **The Church and Education**
"Why They Loved Graceland: In Anticipation" (June 13, 1942): 12.
"Report: New Church School Material" (March 10, 1958): 4.
"Report: New Church School Curriculum for Children and Youth" (June 19, 1961): 4.
"The Church Looks at Weekday Religious Education" (June 19, 1961): 4.
"Education and Spiritual Power," an address at the Kirtland Conference of High Priests (December 1, 1965): 16; reprinted in *Restoration Witness* (September 1966): 2.
"On Being Guest Professor at Graceland" (March 1, 1983): 7.
"Senior Adult Hostel held at Graceland" (March 1, 1985): 14.

Saints Herald: **World Conference Sermons and Reports**
"Our Opportunity for Greatness" (June 15, 1966): 6.
"Report on the Work of the Basic Beliefs Committee" (October 1, 1967): 5.
"Basic Beliefs Committee" (January 1, 1968): 3.
"The Church of Jesus Christ Confronting Its Mission," given at the 1968 World Conference but not published.
"Report of the Basic Beliefs Committee" (March 1970): 6.
"The Great Witnesses," excerpts from the 1970 World Conference address (September 1970): 14.
"Name of the Church Committee Report" (March 1972): 5.
"Called into This Time" (June 1972): 10.

"The Cause of Zion Today and Tomorrow" (August 1974): 10; and (September 1974): 14; chosen for the Elbert A. Smith Memorial Award in 1974.
"On Being the Body of Christ" (August 1976): 16.
"On Choosing Life" (November 1978): 16; and (December 1978): 16.
"Poised Between Eras" (June 1980): 6.
"I Know that My Redeemer Liveth," the 1980 World Conference Communion address (April 1, 1981): 7.
"Report from the Committee on Ministry of the Ordained and Unordained" (February 1982): 29.

Saints Herald: "Into All the World" and "The Twelve Report"

"The 1970s—A Decade of Promise" (February 1970): 7.
"In Memory of Paul Hanson" (August 1972): 6.
"Thanks Be Unto God" (December 1974): 6.
"Asia-Pacific Conference" (June 1975): 6.
"Ministry to the Under 20s" (September 1975): 6.
"World Scouting Development" (February 1976): 8.
"Anticipation of the World Conference" (March 1976): 6.
"Missionary Development Section of the Budget" (May 1976): 38.
"Second Asia-Pacific Conference Scheduled" (January 1977): 6.
"Missions Abroad Education Fund" (February 1977): 6.
"Family Tradition" (March 1977): 6.
"What Does Your Family Mean to You?" (December 1977): 6.
"Good News from the South" (January 1979): 32.
"Good News from the Field" (February 1979): 32.
"The Twelve Report" (March 1979): 32.
"A Need Develops in the Missions Abroad Education Fund" (May 1979).

"Our Children" (October 1979): 32.
"Preparatory Statement to Article in the Council of Twelve Section" (April 1980): 32.

Restoration Witness
"The Christ of the Kingdom" (December 1964): 8.
"Apostle's Testimony" (April 1967): 8.
"Apostle's Testimony" (December 1967): 8.

Priesthood and Leaders Journal
"Ministry to Girls in a Changing World" (November 1961): 36.
"The Department of Religious Education Moves Forward" (December 1964).

Guidelines to Leadership
"These Things Have Worked" (April–June 1945): 10.
"Let the Children See" (December 1953): 20.
"I Have Two Small Sons" (January 1954): 1.
"Mr. Priesthood, Meet Johnny" (January 1954): 6.
"Handwork for Children" (February 1954): 22.
"Your Children Prepare for Baptism" (March 1954): 20.
"Camping for Children" (April 1954): 12.
"A Letter to Church School Supervisors and Teachers" (September 1954): 2.
"Your Department of Religious Education" (September 1954): 1.
"The Department of Religious Education Moves" (November 1954): 11.
"Let's Make Lesson Plans" (December 1954); 16.
"Teacher, This Will Help" (January 1955): 1.
"Real Helps in Memorizing Scriptures" (February 1955): 16.
"Your Church Has Senior Adults" (February 1955): 16.

"A Testing Program for Church School" (December 1955): 14.
"It's General Conference Time" (April 1956): 1.
"Trends in Religious Education" (May 1956): 1.
"Your Branch and Religious Education" (October 1956): 18.
"What a Question Can Do" (November 1956): 27.
"How to Ask a Question" (January 1957): 27.
"Who Is Preparing for Your Job" (February 1957): 8.
"Get the Best Teachers in Your Branch" (March 1957): 1.
"Annual Religious Education Report" (October 1957): 19.
"Letter to Pastors and Church School Directors" (November 1957): 6.
"Annual Religious Education Report" (Summer 1958): 27.
"Letter to the Church" (September 1958): 5.
"Letter to Friends of the Department of Religious Education" (October 1958): 8.
"The Church and Children's Camping" (October 1958): 15.
"Changes in the Department of Religious Education" (February 1959): 7.

Stride

"The Power of Godliness" (June 1959): 24.
"What Does It Mean to Be Saved?" (July 1961): 10.

Commission

"The World Church: Our Mission in the 1980s" (September 1979): 41.

Questions Answered

Concerning selection of presiding officers, *Saints' Herald* (November 9, 1953): 20.

Concerning the addressing of prayers, *Saints' Herald* (July 12, 1954): 18.

Concerning Jesus' education, *Saints' Herald* (August 2, 1954): 11.

Concerning Christ's birthdate, *Question Time, Volume 1* (1955), 11.

Concerning baptism of a woman without permission of husband, *Saints' Herald* (March 27, 1957): 16.

Concerning sanctification, *Saints' Herald* (April 7, 1958): 18.

Concerning Adam's transgression, *Question Time, Volume 3* (1976), 36.

Concerning sacraments and ordinances, *Question Time, Volume 3* (1976), 145.

Concerning service of the Lord's Supper, *Question Time, Volume 3* (1976), 175.

Concerning John the Baptist, *Saints Herald* (December 1979): 29.

"Is the Church Dying?" *Saints Herald* (December 1979): 29.

Concerning succession in the Presidency, *Saints Herald* (December 1979): 29.

Concerning financial law response, *Saints Herald* (December 1979): 29.

Concerning use of the Inspired Version, *Saints Herald* (February 1980): 33.

Unpublished Papers from Joint Council and Other Settings

"The Church as Mission to Society," presented at a conference of women (November 1969).

"The Theology of Mission," an address to high priests and spouses (March 20, 1971).

"The Scriptural and Historical View of Zion," Joint Council seminar (December 1974).

"The Prophetic Voice: Called into Mission" (May 1975).
"On Being a World Church" (July 1975).
"The Patriarch as a Member of the Team," Order of Evangelists workshop (1977).
"Alternative Concepts of the Institutional Church as It Functions Worldwide," Joint Council seminar (December 1976).
"Meaning of the Church as Leaven," Joint Council seminar (March 1977).
"The Evolution of Evangelism in the 60s and 70s," Theology Commission meeting (September 1980).
"Foundations for Contemporary Evangelism" (n.d.).
"A Philosophy for Regional Administration" (n.d.).
"The Church as Mission to Society" (n.d.).
"The Doctrine of the Church" (n.d.).
"The Church of Jesus Christ Confronting Its Mission" (n.d.).